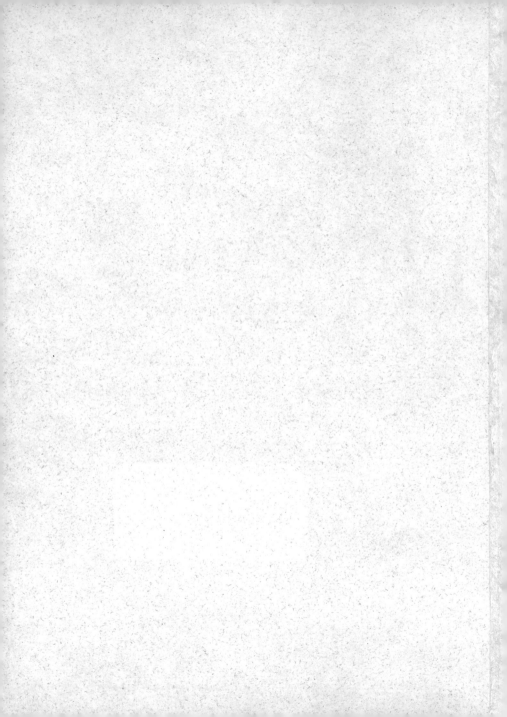

SACRED UNION

Scriptural Keys to

SACRED UNION

a Celestial Marriage

GARY G. TAYLOR

DESERET BOOK COMPANY
SALT LAKE CITY, UTAH

Library of Congress Cataloging-in-Publication Data
Taylor, Gary G.
   Sacred union : scriptural keys to a celestial marriage / Gary Taylor.
    p.   cm.
   Includes bibliographical references and index.
   ISBN 1-57345-492-3 (hardcover)
   1. Marriages—Religious aspects—Church of Jesus Christ of Latter-day Saints.   2. Church of Jesus Christ of Latter-day Saints—Doctrines.   I. Title.
   BX8641.T285   1999
   248.8'44—dc21   99-10514
                                              CIP

Printed in the United States of America

10 9 8 7 6 5 4 3 2 1   72082 - 6453

To Melody

CONTENTS

———

INTRODUCTION

Recently I had a little time and a television remote control in my hand.
Responding to the relentless pressure
from my Y chromosome, I began to channel surf, stopping for a time to hear an impassioned plea from an
expert on marriage. She strongly advocated laws that
would require training before marriage licenses are
issued. She made the familiar point that marriage is
one of the most complex and difficult ventures we can
undertake, yet we allow a couple to marry legally, and
even reproduce, without any training at all.

Certainly the institution of marriage has tremen-
dous impact on our individual and collective well-
being, particularly if children are a product of the
marriage. Yet no training is required. Would we as a
society authorize a person to perform brain surgery if
we were not convinced of the individual's training and

qualifications? Would we grant driving privileges to someone without requiring proof of ability to handle a vehicle safely? Of course not.

Even though passionate and persuasive herself, and even though her assessment of the importance of marriage was accurate, I found myself feeling uneasy about this expert's suggestion. For one thing, if the state required certification before marriage, who would do the training and what course material would be used? The marriage expert I was listening to had written several books on the subject and had developed a series of training classes that she thought would fill the bill nicely.

But there seems to be no end to experts on marriage, and books on the subject fill whole sections in libraries. How can we know what the best option is among the many available? Beyond that, is there any good evidence that marriage experts and their various teachings actually improve marriages? Some who provide premarriage training cite studies showing lower divorce rates among their graduates than in the population at large. But these are correlation studies that do not reveal cause and effect. Isn't it likely that those willing to participate in premarriage instruction are the kind of people who are more likely to be successful in marriage, with or without training?

The fact is, as advice on how to be married has

proliferated, divorce rates have skyrocketed. Current divorce rates have leveled off somewhat from highs in the 1980s, but they are still twice as high as they were in 1960. And rates in 1960 were awful. Though instruction is undoubtedly helpful in some situations, it appears that the solution must lie somewhere other than in premarital training and self-help books.

No one can deny that marriages too often fail, at great expense to everyone involved; and too many of the marriages that survive are not fulfilling. If marriage experts don't have the complete solution to this significant problem, where do we look? I believe the answer has been here all along. I believe the marriage manual we need exists. It's found in the Bible, the oldest and most frequently published book in history. It's found in other ancient scriptures brought to light by a prophet in our day—the Book of Mormon and the Pearl of Great Price. It's found in the Doctrine and Covenants and other writings and words of current prophets and apostles. The scriptures provide the best marriage manual available; and couples will be the happiest, families the most secure, and society the winner if the precepts taught in scripture are understood and followed.

I expect that most readers will agree with this general premise, and I hope that many readers of this book are well versed in the scriptures. Yet how to make practical application of scriptural directives regarding family relationships is not always understood, or at least not carefully done. As an example, a man I know is a Church member with a long history of comprehensive gospel study. When I first met him, he could quote chapter and verse on any number of subjects. Even so, his marriage was in shambles, and his relationship with his children was abysmal.

This man, whom I will call Matt, was a perfectionist. His favorite scripture seemed to be Matthew 5:48: "Be ye therefore perfect." In his interpretation, the directive to be perfect meant things such as have a perfect yard, have impeccable manners, and never waste time. His standards were extremely high, and probably unreasonable, but that wasn't the problem. The problem was the impatient, critical, and even brutal way he reacted to his wife and children when they fell short of his standards. (Incidentally, Matt often fell short too, although he would rarely admit it.)

Several bishops and a marriage counselor had tried valiantly to explain to Matt that he needed to strive to be perfect in tolerance, patience, long-suffering and love, as well as be perfect in carrying out assignments and duties. In fact, the scriptures (1 Corinthians 13:1-3, for example) point out that charity, the pure love of Christ, is the most important virtue of all. Unfortunately, Matt just didn't get it. He persisted in blaming his wife and children for the problems in his family. In his mind, all would be well if they would simply follow his directives. After all, wasn't he the priesthood leader in the home and didn't he want only the best for his family?

Suggestions from Matt's Church leaders and his counselor to back off and be more patient were outrightly rejected. He viewed such advice as softheaded at best. At worst, it was the result of his wife's manipulation of those giving the advice. He thought that her whining had somehow won these advisers over to her view of things. Matt's number one job was to get his family to the celestial kingdom, and he was absolutely convinced that they needed to be prodded, not coddled. He was overlooking the fact that no one can be forced to heaven. Righteous goals can be pursued only in righteousness (see D&C 21:36–38).

In effect, Matt had heard the word of the Lord, but he wasn't really following it. And, unfortunately, his failure to truly understand and follow God's marriage manual led to an ugly divorce, resulting in abundant pain and suffering for all involved. His relationship with his children deteriorated to the point that they lost respect for their father. Because of this, not only did he lose his family, he lost the opportunity to influence them, which was, ironically, his primary goal in the first place.

Matt's is a classic example of what the Lord warned us about when he said: "He that receiveth my law and doeth it, the same is my disciple; and he that saith he receiveth it and doeth it not, the same is not my disciple, and shall be cast out from among you" (D&C 41:5). Matt, and all of us, must be "doers of the word, and not hearers only" (James 1:22). Otherwise, as James goes on to say, we end up deceiving ourselves and suffering the consequences.

God's marriage manual points out that, along with charity, other virtues such as forgiveness, humility, honesty, and fidelity are critically important in family relationships. In this book I have selected a few of the many basic directives found in scripture and have attempted to illustrate how they apply in our marriage and family relationships. In doing so, I do not claim to speak for God. We know that He is perfectly capable of speaking for Himself. The problem is that we sometimes aren't very good at listening. I hope that the examples provided here will motivate the reader to listen, to ponder relevant scriptures, and to look for the correct application in his or her life. We have the perfect marriage manual available, and with some effort and humility on our part, we can have it personally interpreted for us by the Spirit of God. There is no better training opportunity in the universe.

CHAPTER ONE

FORGIVE ONE ANOTHER

―――――

Then came Peter to him, and said, Lord, how oft shall my brother sin against me, and I forgive him? till seven times? Jesus saith unto him, I say not unto thee, Until seven times, But, Until seventy times seven.

MATTHEW 18:21-22

Doing the math on the Lord's directive results in a large number. Forgiving 490 times sounds like a challenge. Even more challenging, the Lord's comment is generally understood to suggest that we should be continually forgiving, no matter how often we are offended. Furthermore, the scriptures teach that we should forgive major as well as minor offenses. As reported in the 50th chapter of Genesis, Joseph successfully met the challenge of forgiving brothers who had sought his life and ultimately sold him into slavery. Fortunately, not too many of us have to deal with an offense of that magnitude.

After many years and much suffering because of their treatment of him, Joseph and his brothers were reunited. By this time, Joseph had gained a position of power in Egypt and his brothers were at his mercy. Once Joseph revealed his identity, his brothers pleaded for forgiveness: "Forgive, I pray thee now, the trespass of thy brethren, and their sin; for they did unto thee evil: and now, we pray thee, forgive the trespass of the servants of the God of thy father" (Genesis 50:17). Joseph might have been full of bitterness and anger after so many years, and he might have relished the opportunity he now had to make them suffer as he had. But to his brothers he said, "Now therefore fear ye not: I will nourish you, and your little ones. And he comforted them, and spake kindly unto them" (Genesis 50:21). This is a classic example of someone following the imperative given in God's marriage manual that we forgive even serious offenses.

Instructions to forgive and examples of forgiveness are found throughout scripture and cover all ages of time. It's a very old principle. Yet modern researchers and health professionals are just now coming on board. Forgiveness has only recently become a popular subject for psychological study, and there is even a Forgiveness Summit being planned to ring in the year 2000. And what are the findings of the current research being done on forgiveness?

Willingness to forgive others seems to be good for us. This conclusion isn't surprising to the person of faith who might wonder why it takes scientific research to discover something so basic.

That same person of faith, however, may still have trouble applying the principle, especially in family situations. As with other virtues, this one is easy to talk about, but not so easy to apply.

WHAT IS FORGIVENESS?

As outlined below, there are three basic elements involved in forgiveness:

How We Act

How do we behave in our relationships with those who offend us? To be forgiving in our actions means to avoid trying to get even. It means treating the other person well in spite of how we have been treated.

How We Feel

How do we feel when thinking about or when in the presence of someone who has offended us? To forgive at an emotional level means that we can think about or be in the presence of those who have offended us without becoming angry, hurt, or defensive.

How We Think

What do we think of those who have offended us? To truly forgive means to hope the best for that person rather than thinking evil of the offender. It means to focus on the positive and not the negative aspects of those who offend us.

It's important to note that losing or suppressing memory of the offense is not an integral part of forgiving those who offend us. Somewhere along the line, someone coined the phrase "forgive and forget." It's entirely possible, however, to forgive without forgetting. In fact, some things may never be forgotten, but we can come to peace with them even so. Joseph in the Old Testament certainly had not forgotten what his brothers had done to him, but he was still able to treat them well, find emotional peace in the situation, and have his brothers' best interest at heart.

The possibility of losing the pain in the memory but still remembering the offense is described beautifully by the prophet Alma in the Book of Mormon. In this case, Alma needed to forgive himself. He was "racked with torment" and "harrowed up" by the memory of sins committed in his youth (see Alma 36:17). The pain continued until he realized that he could be forgiven through the atonement of Christ. With this understanding, the memory of his sins continued, but the associated emotional pain did not. "And now, behold, when I thought this, I could remember my pains no more; yea, I was harrowed up by the memory of my sins no more. And oh, what joy, and what marvelous light I did behold; yea, my soul was filled with joy as exceeding as was my pain!" (Alma 36:19-20).

Alma's description makes the point nicely that when we forgive, either another or ourselves, we may remember the offense, but we are not troubled by the memory. It no longer affects our actions or our feelings. It no longer results in negative thoughts. We may continue to be affected by the offense at some level, but the matter has ceased to cause us pain. We are at peace.

ROUTINE FORGIVENESS IN FAMILY RELATIONSHIPS

As an example of how forgiveness works at a more mundane level, we were upgrading our house, and I had spent a great deal of time painting. I had overdosed on painting by the time we got to a guest bedroom, and since the original paint was still in reasonably good condition, my wife and I made a mutual decision to leave it as it was. Later, she decided that she would just touch the room up a bit. The new paint seemed to match the old paint, but once dry and in better light, the room looked as though it had contracted chicken pox.

This was irritating to me, but matters got even worse. When she put the can of paint back in the garage, my wife left it on the edge of the counter and didn't secure the lid. Later on, while in the garage, I accidentally brushed the can, and it fell on the floor, spilling almost a gallon of paint.

We have probably all experienced something similar at one time or another. When we do, we face a test of character. The first question is how will we respond to such provocations? The sad truth is that people have committed murder over simple problems such as this, and the use of profane language isn't all that uncommon. To forgive, of course, means to respond without rancor: "No problem. I know it wasn't intentional. It could happen to anyone." (I'll leave it to the reader to guess how I responded!)

Another aspect of forgiveness has to do with our emotions. How am I feeling? To forgive means that I resolve any anger resulting from the offense and that I maintain or restore positive feelings toward the one offending me. In this scenario, if I can clean up the paint, get rid of any anger about the incident, and go to my wife with good feelings toward her, I have passed this part of the character test.

The last level is cognitive. What am I thinking? Am I thinking how careless my wife was and how unnecessary all of this is? Do I attack her in my mind? Do I ponder ways to teach her a lesson? Am I feeling sorry for myself? Or do I strive to school my feelings by thinking less about the inconvenience it is to me and more about how my wife must feel? The interesting thing is that what I allow myself to think about the situation dictates how I will behave and what my emotional state will be. If I am to truly forgive, my thoughts must be forgiving. I won't have much luck acting in a forgiving manner, or obtaining emotional peace in the situation, if my thinking remains hostile and negative.

WHY IS IT SO HARD?

There are a number of reasons we have trouble forgiving. One of the most common is the worry that we may be letting the other person get away with offensive behavior. This is what seemed to be going on in the case of Ruth and her lukewarm-in-the-priesthood husband. Ruth had married a returned missionary in the temple and thought that by doing so, achieving one of her important goals in life would be a given. Ruth believed that her husband would help her maintain a strong spiritual atmosphere in their home.

Unfortunately, it didn't turn out that way. After several years of marriage, Richard was active in the Church, but at a marginal level. If the family had prayer together or a family home evening, Ruth had to engineer it. Richard also saw nothing wrong with engaging in recreational activities on Sunday, such as eating out with the family. Ruth made it very clear to Richard that she was not comfortable with that kind of Sunday activity; but one day after church, Richard suggested in front of the kids that they all go out for ice cream. You can imagine the children's response. This put Ruth in an uncomfortable, no-win situation. If she stuck to her principles, she was the bad guy, and if she went along with Richard, she would be condoning an activity she felt was inappropriate.

Ruth was livid. She tore into her husband for being so insensitive, doing so in front of the children. She stormed out of the room and refused to speak to Richard except in monosyllables for several days. Her mind was preoccupied with thoughts about how unfair Richard had been in this instance, but also how unfair he had been in general. In her mind, he had deceived her. She felt as though he had pretended to be strong in the Church before they married, but that he really wasn't. In short, Ruth was not forgiving on all three levels discussed previously.

When it was suggested that she needed to forgive Richard for the ice cream incident—as well as for all other disappointments in the past, present, and future—she balked. She was familiar with the scriptural requirement, but couldn't bring herself to forgive. She was afraid that forgiving Richard would equate to endorsing his behavior.

She reasoned that if she were to forgive him for things such as the Sunday ice cream, he would be more likely to do that and even more objectionable things in the future. The danger was that if she gave an inch, he would take a mile. It wasn't so much that she was trying to punish him for his offenses, but rather that she was trying to get him to change in order to prevent this kind of thing in the future. Either way, the result of her not following the Lord's marriage manual was the same. She was miserable, she was contributing to problems in her marriage, and she was not setting a good example for her children.

When she finally realized the harm her behavior was causing, she decided that she needed to do the right thing, no matter the consequence. If by forgiving him she was reinforcing the kind of behavior that offended her, so be it. It was unfair that Richard wasn't doing his share spiritually. What's more, he had hurt her by being insensitive to her heartfelt requests about Sunday activities; but she was hurting herself much more by failing to forgive. Her example and influence in the family had become negative, and she was not helping Richard.

If there were anything she could do to help him with his commitment, it would be that she honor hers. In baptism she had committed to keep the Lord's commandments. High on the list of those commandments is the requirement to love, be long-suffering, and practice charity. If she could continue to set an example on the letter of the law issues *and* show love and charity to her husband, who knows? Maybe he would come around. But if not, at least she would be doing her part to make things right, while at the same time not making things worse.

Ruth's plan was to continue to organize family prayer and home evenings, even though Richard wasn't doing his part. She would politely decline to go out for Sunday ice cream or participate in similar activities, giving her reasons for not going, but she wouldn't attack her husband or children for their interest in doing so. She would also do what she could to head off potential Sabbath conflicts by making sure ice cream treats and meaningful family activities were available at home. When Ruth did need to confront Richard and seek his cooperation, she would do it in the spirit of a forgiving attitude, rather than in a confrontational, holier-than-thou manner. Not surprisingly, Ruth found this approach to be infinitely more effective. It worked better both in terms of how it made Ruth feel and in her family's coming closer to her ideal.

And where did Ruth find this strategy? It was in God's marriage manual all along. Jesus taught: "My disciples, in days of old, sought occasion against one another [probably for what they considered to be righteous reasons] and forgave not one another in their hearts; and for this evil they were afflicted and sorely chastened. Wherefore, I say unto you, that ye ought to forgive one another; for he that forgiveth not his brother his trespasses standeth condemned before the Lord; for there remaineth in him the greater sin. I, the Lord, will forgive whom I will forgive, but of you it is required to forgive all men" (D & C 64:8–10).

Ruth realized that no matter how offensive she thought her husband's weaknesses were, or how disruptive to family spiritual goals, the greater sin for her would be to fail to forgive. That would compound the consequences of her husband's error while adding a large measure of negative consequences from her own mistake.

As a side note, some readers may question the doctrine that failing to forgive is a greater sin than the sin we are loath to forgive. Does that mean that if someone kills my child and I fail to forgive that I am worse than a murderer? Not likely. On a scale of sins, murder no doubt ranks higher (see D&C 42:18). It is not a matter of ranking sinful behavior. What I must realize is that when I am offended by someone, the only thing for which I am responsible, and the only thing that can affect me emotionally and spiritually on into the future, is how I respond. In that sense, failure to forgive is undoubtedly the greatest sin for me.

Likewise, whether or not she would forgive her husband was the only thing in the above situation that Ruth could control. Therefore, not forgiving would be the greater sin for her, no matter where her husband's mistakes ranked on a scale of sins. Interestingly, in Ruth's case, her husband was actually pretty good at showing patience, being long-suffering, and demonstrating love. His shortcomings were in the area of fulfilling assignments and taking care of his duties. Until Ruth made the change described above, her problems were just the reverse. In other words, they both needed to change, and, therefore, it's probably a moot point to debate whose sins were the worst.

Before leaving Ruth's example, it's worth noting that she was also guilty of coveting, as will be discussed in chapter four. True, what she was coveting was something righteous, i.e., to have a "celestial family." Yet when we covet something so badly that we can't be happy without it, we can get in trouble no matter how worthy the goal. This is especially true when what we desire is beyond our control. Ruth had a picture in her mind of how her husband and her family should operate. She desired fulfillment of that dream more than anything else. Unfortunately, she wanted it so badly she couldn't be happy without it. When her husband and children didn't cooperate with her dream, she was guilty of resorting to unforgiving, manipulative behavior.

I WON'T LET HIM GET AWAY WITH IT!

Ruth's example is a case in which forgiveness was blocked by a need to stand on principle. A related obstacle to forgiveness is the perceived need to stand up for oneself. Sometimes forgiving (turning the other cheek) seems like a weak act that undermines personal integrity. Symptomatic of this attitude is the comment: "I refuse to allow myself to be treated that way!"

A father and son experienced this kind of problem. One evening a particularly ugly incident occurred. It began with an argument over a poor report card. The son was defensive and soon became hostile and profane, swearing at his father. His father shouted back, "I refuse to let you talk to me that way" and came at his son. They scuffled a bit, yelled at each other, and Dad then stomped off, realizing that things had gotten badly out of hand. Even though Dad recognized the problem, there was no immediate forgiveness in his heart as he kept thinking how unreasonable his son was and how a father shouldn't have to stand for that kind of insolence. But with the passage of a little time, his attitude softened, and the first stirrings of forgiveness were felt.

This change was encouraged as he pondered Paul's comment in Ephesians 6:4: "And, ye fathers, provoke not your children to wrath: but bring them up in the nurture and admonition of the Lord." Dad recognized that, no matter how he had been provoked, he had not handled the situation in a way acceptable to the Lord.

For his part, the son continued to stew, resenting the way his father had treated him. Pride and anger led him to pack a bag and storm out of the house, stating that he was leaving and never coming back. A friend came to pick him up, and he left, leaving a tearful Mom protesting and pleading that he stay and work things out.

Having cooled off himself, Dad followed his son to the bus station, and as the boy boarded the bus,

Dad was able to say, "Son, I know that I've made mistakes, but I love you. Please forgive me."

As the bus carried him away from his home, the son kept hearing his father's words: "Son, I love you, please forgive me." As he reflected on those words, a spirit of forgiveness entered his heart also, and, at the next stop, he purchased a ticket home, returning late that night. He entered the home to find his father sitting in a chair in the living room, slumped in grief. All the son had to say was, "Dad," and they ran into each other's arms.

The willingness to forgive one another eventually saved the day in this situation, although it was long in coming because of that all-too-human tendency to "refuse to be treated that way," which is to say that we are often prevented from forgiving others due to one of the other human faults we are warned about in God's marriage manual. I suppose we like to think we are simply standing up for ourselves, or refusing to be a doormat, when we refuse to be treated a certain way. But, as will be discussed later, it is pride that stands in our way, preventing us from behaving nobly, inducing us instead to be stubborn, pig-headed, and foolish!

Even so, I don't believe that the Lord's marriage manual requires that anyone should be a doormat. One can be a forgiving person without being a pushover. We can give our opinion, we can ask for cooperation, and we can refuse to go along with unacceptable requests. We can stick up for our values, beliefs, and wishes. We can do all of this and still be a forgiving person, if we do so without attacking those who offend us and if we don't *demand* that they modify their behavior. We certainly can ask, but we can't insist on behavior change. If our requests are ignored, we may need to modify *our* behavior in order to protect ourselves in certain situations. An abused wife, for example, may need to move to a protected environment and ultimately file for divorce. But there is no provision in the gospel to justify the use of force in trying to modify another's behavior.

In the situation between the father and his son, Dad needed to respond in some way that would maintain his integrity as the father, without making matters worse. He might have applied a consequence for his son's misbehavior, such as: "That outburst just cost you use of the car for the weekend!" Or Dad might have expressed his disappointment and hurt at being treated so poorly by his son, and simply walked out of the room. Neither response would have been a personal attack on his son, nor would either have been a *demand* that his son change. In fact, Dad could have done a number of things that might have influenced his son to be reasonable, any of which would have been appropriate. But Dad could not *demand* that his son stop swearing, unless he was willing to back it up with physical force. Unfortunately, that's exactly what happened.

Naturally, this rule about not insisting that another modify his or her behavior gets fuzzy when dealing with dependent children. In that case, parents have the responsibility to try to influence and change the improper behavior of their offspring. But even here, a forgiving attitude, such as the one illustrated above, is vitally important. Parents can and should set limits and impose natural and logical consequences when their children make mistakes. On the other hand, condemning a child personally, seeking vengeance, harboring negative thoughts, or resorting to any form of abuse is clearly destructive. And all of these destructive responses grow out of an unforgiving attitude.

IT MUST BE FAIR AND JUST

A third common obstacle to forgiving is the trouble we typically have accepting something that isn't fair. We want to see justice done. Some form of righteous indignation usually wells up and makes it hard to make the truly righteous choice to forgive. We are not satisfied that the Lord will mete out justice in

His own due time. We want justice according to our time frame, which is usually right now!

Let's say you reveal something private about yourself to your husband or wife, such as the fact that you are self-conscious about the shape of your nose. Then at a dinner party the subject of vanity and plastic surgery comes up, and your partner reveals to the group the concern you have about your appearance and your secret desire to have plastic surgery. Further, let's say the comment is made in a joking way, sending the message that you are silly for having this concern. That would clearly be a betrayal of confidence by your partner, and you would likely find the breach of loyalty offensive and humiliating.

How would you grant forgiveness in such a situation? Certainly it would be appropriate to privately express how much the betrayal of confidence hurt you. God's marriage manual teaches us the need to clearly identify the problem to whomever offends us whenever we are offended. For example, in Matthew 18:15, we read: "Moreover if thy brother shall trespass against thee, go and tell him his fault between thee and him alone: if he shall hear thee, thou hast gained thy brother." Again, this works better if our attitude is forgiving and not accusatory when we raise our complaint.

Ultimately, however, forgiveness involves the three

aspects outlined earlier. You would need to forgive *behaviorally*, which means to avoid mistreating your partner for the way he or she mistreated you. Second, you need to forgive *emotionally*, which means finding a degree of peace in the situation so that you can feel good about yourself and about your partner. (Not necessarily about your partner's behavior at the dinner party.) Third, you need to *think* positively about your partner, focusing on the good he or she does, instead of on the mistake that was made.

All of this is hard to do because the whole thing just isn't fair. You, of course, would never do something like that to your partner (which probably isn't true, but it always seems like it when we are the victims of something like this). Not only that, but likely as not, you won't get a proper apology. Let's say that in the above situation, you express how the comment hurt, and your partner embraces you and tearfully admits the mistake and begs your forgiveness. That would be nice, but what are the chances?

More likely you'll get a defensive response, something like, "I'm sorry you were upset by that. I didn't mean to put you down. I think you are just too sensitive." Now it's *really* unfair! Not only has your partner done something awful to you that you would never do to him or her, but your partner is refusing to take responsibility and, in effect, blaming you for the problem. "You're just too sensitive."

To forgive in this situation, as in most, means enduring something that isn't fair. Typically we don't deserve whatever hurt us, and usually the apology and request for forgiveness from the offender is not up to our expectations. Yet God's marriage manual requires that we forgive anyway. In God's book it's clear that offenders are not excused. They must rectify their negative behavior and stand accountable for it. But victims are still required to forgive. Otherwise, the unfairness is multiplied. When we fail to forgive, we make a bad situation worse. We compound the pain that is inevitable in hurtful situations, and we block the quickest path to emotional resolution.

HELPS IN FORGIVING

Forgiving others at the most basic level requires us to make a series of behavioral adjustments. Three of the necessary adjustments have already been outlined. (1) We must avoid insisting on fairness and leave justice to the Lord. (2) We need to do the right thing, even if doing so seems to let the other person get away with it. (3) We must avoid making demands that others change their behavior or opinions, even if they are wrong. These are simple to describe, but hard to do when it comes time to follow through. Usually we have to remind ourselves repeatedly of our resolve and work hard to keep our commitment.

Beyond these basic efforts, it also helps to choose carefully where we focus our thoughts. It's natural when offended to pursue fantasies and daydreams of getting even or to go over and over the offense in our mind, reveling almost in the rehearsal and fueling additional resentment. In fact, there are some professionals who suggest that we should relive the offense through emotional review, letter writing, role-playing, or some other means in order to resolve the pain. But I believe that the Lord's way is infinitely superior. We need to look away rather than stage a fight. We need to focus on what's right in the world, not what's wrong.

In numerous places (for example, Matthew 17:21) God's marriage manual also counsels us that we seek spiritual help through prayer when faced with a challenge. Abby had such a challenge with the principle of forgiveness. As a child, she had been repeatedly sexually molested by her father. She suffered all of the usual problems experienced by victims of this kind of outrage; and it took her years to deal with the resulting issues. One of these issues was the hatred she felt for her father. Her father's problem and his inability to come to grips with it, meant that Abby would never in this life be able to be close to him, which was an enormous disappointment for her. But Abby could deal with that. What she couldn't deal with was the hatred she felt. That went with her into all aspects of her life and robbed her of peace of mind.

Abby found that with effort she was able to forgive her father on a behavioral level. She wisely kept her distance from him, and she treated him courteously when interaction was necessary at family gatherings. She found it hard, however, to forgive him cognitively and emotionally. Her thoughts toward him were hostile and mean-spirited, and whenever she thought about him or whenever she was in his presence, it was an emotional nightmare for her.

Resolution in Abby's case was the result of her making her best effort and getting help from the Lord. At first, she only prayed for help with her problem, while putting little effort into controlling her thoughts about her father. Her anger persisted. Later, after she had somewhat given up on prayer, she tried to solve the problem on her own, by carefully monitoring her thoughts. Still the problem persisted. It wasn't until she gave it her best effort, *and* prayed fervently that the goal was realized. In her words, "It was like a weight being released. I suddenly felt free. I could think about my father without emotion. I recognized the evil for which he was responsible, but I was able to sincerely pray for his welfare. I couldn't have done that on my own. I believe it was a gift." And so it was. Forgiving those who commit serious sin toward us is not easy, and it's comforting to know that the Lord's help is available when our own best efforts fall short.

I hope Abby's description of what she felt after learning to forgive will motivate any reader with a similar need. It really is worth the effort, and there is no better solution. By granting forgiveness to those who have offended us, much of the anger we might experience in our family relationships, as described in the next chapter, can be overcome.

CHAPTER TWO

RELEASE ANGER

———

A wrathful man stirreth up strife: but he
that is slow to anger appeaseth strife.

PROVERBS 15:18

The Lord's marriage manual has a lot to say about anger, which is a subject closely related to the principle of forgiveness. Anger is usually involved when we have trouble forgiving, and the disappearance of anger is an indication that we have succeeded in forgiving. Regarding anger, we learn in the scriptures that ultimately it has a positive form and expression. For instance, there are several references in the scriptures to God's anger being directed toward evil and unrighteousness. There is also the instance in which Jesus made a scourge of small cords and drove moneychangers from the temple (see John 2:13–17). For mortals, however, anger is usually characterized as negative.

Human anger is variously described as a curse (see Genesis 49:7) or as foolish (see Proverbs 14:17).

Frequently it is referred to as being instigated by Satan (see Moroni 9:3; 3 Nephi 11:29). This last reference is particularly on point. "For verily, verily I say unto you, he that hath the spirit of contention is not of me, but is of the devil, who is the father of contention, and he stirreth up the hearts of men to contend with anger, one with another. Behold, this is not my doctrine, to stir up the hearts of men with anger, one against another; but this is my doctrine, that such things should be done away" (3 Nephi 11:29–30).

These scripture references, and our own common experience, suggest that anger is something to be controlled and managed. It rarely has a positive effect in family relationships. An angry outburst might get the attention of your spouse or children, and they might in fact obey your wishes for a time. But when changes are coerced, they are never heartfelt and are, therefore, likely to be short-lived. To keep control, you may end up having to blow up again and again.

Angry responses also tend to take the focus away from the offender's culpability and place it on the angry victim. For example, a spouse who makes a mistake and is angrily attacked for it may be so affected by the angry outburst that he or she will fail to focus on the mistake that led to the anger in the first place. A less angry confrontation is more likely to result in the one who made the mistake recognizing the fact and accepting responsibility for it.

One of the reasons we sometimes have trouble getting past anger is the common but mistaken notion that unexpressed or bottled anger is somehow dangerous. Anger is thought of as a force that builds up in a person and must be vented before it becomes explosive. The idea is that we need to "get our anger out." Repressed anger is also believed by many to cause various emotional and physical problems. In recent years, depression, colitis, ulcers, and being overweight have all been blamed on suppressed anger. There are also those who feel that angry outbursts are a form of honesty. They may say, "I'm not trying to hurt you; I'm just honestly sharing my feelings." The assumption is that to do otherwise would somehow be dishonest.

Happily, current research generally discredits the old notion that suppressing anger is dangerous. We now know that ulcers are not caused by the suppression of anger. Nor is there a link, as once thought, between obesity and repressed anger. Actually, there is no solid evidence of *any* link between health problems and suppressed anger. Research studies suggesting otherwise are typically flawed in ways that make their results meaningless. Furthermore, it has become a little less fashionable to think of venting hostile emotions as somehow noble and cathartic. More often currently, such behavior is labeled as self-centered and destructive—a much more accurate description.

But, whatever the current opinion of psychologists, I believe the truth has been available in God's marriage manual from the beginning. The Lord is quoted as saying, "But I say unto you, That whosoever is angry with his brother *without a cause* shall be in danger of the judgment" (Matthew 5:22; emphasis added). Interestingly, in the Book of Mormon rendition of the same sermon (see 3 Nephi 12:22), the phrase "without a cause" is not found. This suggests the need to control anger, whether or not our anger seems justified.

Clearly, letting loose with angry language and behavior is *not* in our best interest. In venting we keep angry thoughts harrowed up, which simply reinforces the anger, while at the same time we invite a defensive or confrontational response from the one at whom our anger is directed. In addition, we sometimes do silly things in response to anger (i.e., put holes in walls, break things, and say hurtful things we don't really mean). By venting anger we, therefore, often become a double victim. We are victimized by whatever upsets us in the first place and then again by our response to the initial offense. In short, angry responses engender additional anger, damage relationships, and oftentimes lead to foolish or dangerous behavior.

In a conference address given many years ago, Brigham Young told it like it is, in his own direct and colorful style: "When evil arises within me let me throw a cloak over it, subdue it instead of acting it out upon the false presumption that I am honest and no hypocrite. Let not thy tongue give utterance to the evil that is in thine heart, but command thy tongue to be silent until good shall prevail over the evil, until thy wrath has passed away and the good spirit shall move thy tongue to blessings and words of kindness. So far I believe in being a hypocrite. This is practical with me. When my feelings are aroused to anger by the ill-doings of others, I hold them as I would hold a wild horse, and I gain the victory. Some think and say that it makes them feel better when they are mad, as they call it, to give vent to their madness in abusive and unbecoming language. This, however, is a mistake. Instead of its making you feel better, it is making bad worse. When you think and say it makes you better you give credit to a falsehood. When the wrath and bitterness of the human heart are moulded into words and hurled with violence at one another, without any check or hindrance, the fire has no sooner expended itself than it is again re-kindled through some trifling course, until the course of nature is set on fire; 'and it is set on fire in hell'" (*Journal of Discourses* 11:255).

Marriages would be infinitely better if couples followed Brigham's advice by throwing a cloak over their anger and holding their tempers as they would a wild horse. As an example of someone who contradicted this advice, I'm thinking of a young husband who had difficulty controlling his temper. Rather than forgive and look past problems, as described in the previous chapter, Hal would blow up. He could blow up over most anything, but usually his fits were in response to suspected infidelity.

If his wife spent a little too much time talking to another man at church, Hal would fume about her flirting. If his wife seemed to be enjoying the main character in a movie a little too much, Hal would sulk and get upset about her lusting after the movie star. On one occasion his wife smiled a little too warmly at a waiter in a restaurant, and Hal loudly stomped off, leaving his wife at the dinner table to face one of the most embarrassing moments of her life. Hal then spent several days after that in episodic fits of anger before he was able to calm down.

Hal got as angry as he did for some of the reasons discussed above. He felt that he must get his concerns off his chest, almost as if he had a duty to vent his frustrations in order to be honest with his wife, and to preserve his own sanity. But unfortunately, when he vented, he was simply reviewing the incident that caused the anger in the first place, further agitating himself and becoming, in the process, more and more angry. His wife was understandably insulted by his suspicions, and his outbursts invariably spawned an argument between them. In defending his accusations, he reinforced them in his mind, which further fueled his angry feelings.

Hal's anger also reinforced the general paranoia he experienced about his wife. Sometimes the mere fact that he was angry and upset was proof that there must be something to be upset about—a common and quite a vicious circle. Hal's wife also got defensive when he blew up, which Hal interpreted as evidence of her guilt. Furthermore, his wife became sensitive to what might cause Hal's temper to flare, and her resulting awkward behavior looked to Hal like more evidence of wrongdoing. There were also a few incidents in which his wife actually did flirt with other men, in a way just to spite Hal. None of this behavior on his wife's part was justified, but it was almost to be expected based on how Hal treated her.

For his part, Hal blamed his anger on his wife. Whenever he blew up, it was in response to his wife doing something that Hal honestly believed was wrong. That, in his mind, justified his becoming angry. In a way, he was afraid not to be angry, for fear that his wife would then assume that there was nothing wrong with her behavior. (Incidentally, anyone with an anger problem needs to take a good look at this issue. Is the anger being kept alive primarily to make a point and/or control someone else?)

The fact is, Hal's anger was inappropriate whether or not his wife was guilty as charged. By being angry and venting his anger, he became a double victim. He was hurt initially by his perception of his wife's behavior, but hurt much more by his angry response. His anger certainly did nothing to improve the quality of his life, and it caused great turmoil in his marriage. Rather than helping guarantee his wife's fidelity, his anger guaranteed the death of intimacy and warmth in his marriage.

AVOID OPERATING IN ABSOLUTES

Hal's anger originated in his extreme, unrealistic expectations of his wife. Usually anger occurs when something does not happen that we think must or when something does happen that we think must not. That's true much more often than it needs to be for someone like Hal, who thinks in extremes. Such people tend to think in terms of "must," "have to," "can't," "always," and "never." Hal thought that his wife *had to* cease and desist in the behavior that so upset him. A wife who loves her husband would *never* act like that. Hal further thought that his wife *must* understand and agree with his viewpoint. There was absolutely no room for tolerance, acceptance, or forgiveness in Hal's thinking, even though, philosophically, Hal agreed that people should be tolerant, accepting, and forgiving.

All of this put Hal at emotional risk because, as often as not, things don't happen the way they "must," and things do happen that "can't." This seems to be especially true in family relationships, where it is often hard even to get agreement on what the ideal is. If a video of Hal and his wife interacting were to be shown, most observers would probably take the side of Hal's wife in the foregoing example, but others might think that Hal has a point.

Since perceptions and values differ so much between us, not to mention the fact that none of us is perfect, it's inevitable that spouses and children will sometimes disappoint us. And so will moms and dads, aunts and uncles, and everybody else for that matter. Sometimes they will disappoint us because they don't see things the way we do, and other times they will agree with us, but go against our wishes anyway. Those who can't tolerate the disappointment and who try to control others are on dangerous ground, as in the previous example, and as further illustrated by an ugly confrontation between a mother and her son.

This mom asked her teenage son to clean his room, but he refused and swore vilely at her in the process. Mom thought it essential that her son clean his room, and she was angry that he had dared talk to her that way. By responding inflexibly to the situation, she painted herself into a corner emotionally. If her son had apologized and cleaned his room, there would have been no problem. But since he continued to rebel, Mom got more and more angry, raising her voice and finally striking out at him. The son defended himself, and both mother and son were injured in the resulting melee. Giving her son no choice and emotionally demanding that he *must* clean his room and insisting that she *would not* allow him to talk to her that way, both the mother and son endured a very destructive experience. Many cases of domestic violence can be explained, in part, by angry people locking themselves into just such uncompromising positions.

The fact is, the son in this example did *not* have to clean his room and he apparently *could* talk to his mom in that way. His behavior was certainly offensive, but his mother could not *force* him to behave otherwise. If Mom had recognized her son's agency in the matter, she might have been better able to control her anger. By controlling her anger she would then have been more likely to think clearly. She might then have seen that though she couldn't control her son's behavior, she could control the car keys, access to the television and the computer, other privileges, and, ultimately, whether or not her son was welcome to continue living at home.

Applying consequences that she could control might have had a positive impact, but the verbal and physical confrontation clearly did not. In fact, in this case, the son was so preoccupied with reacting to and defending himself from what he saw as an angry overreaction by his mother, that he didn't clearly focus on the fact that his behavior was way out of line.

It's much easier to avoid this kind of situation if we have the perspective taught in the Lord's marriage manual. In the Book of Mormon we read: "Wherefore, men are free according to the flesh; and all things are given them which are expedient unto man. And they are free to choose liberty and eternal life, through the great Mediator of all men, or to choose captivity and death, according to the captivity and power of the devil; for he seeketh that all men might be miserable like unto himself" (2 Nephi 2:27). God doesn't force any of us to behave, but there are consequences that naturally follow both our good and bad choices.

Likewise, we avoid a lot of trouble if we don't demand that others comply with our wishes. They always have a choice, even if their choices are downright evil.

OTHER HELPS IN MANAGING ANGER

As suggested previously, we can help ourselves manage anger by respecting the principle of agency in others. Since we may get frustrated and angry if we use too many "have to's" on ourselves, it also helps to give ourselves sufficient choices. Let's say a dad decides that he *can't* be disturbed as he works on a project at home that he declares *must* be finished that evening. He locks himself in his den, but the loud music from his daughter's room filters through the heating vent, breaking his concentration. Then little Johnny bangs on the door and cries for attention. His wife, who is a little late rescuing Dad from little Johnny, then interrupts with a "sorry to bother you" message that she feels is important. In a family situation, there is pretty much a guarantee that we will be interrupted on any given evening; and given the demands of a "have to" project, the likelihood of our getting angry increases with each interruption.

If this father had given himself more leeway in whether or not his project got finished, meaning that he wasn't under as much pressure to get the job done, the inevitable interruptions would have been less irritating. Unfortunately, that was not possible in this case because of how Dad had set up his evening. He had fallen into the common trap of thinking in absolutes, even when they don't necessarily apply. He had decided he had to get the project completed that evening, but it was not actually a life-and-death issue. In the few cases where absolutes really do apply, planning is required to avoid being rushed and to minimize distractions. Usually that means avoiding attempting to do whatever needs to be accomplished at home with the kids!

In that regard, absolute thinking can make planning difficult. Dad in the example thought he *had to* finish the project, but he also *had to* be home. He felt he had already been out too many nights recently. Furthermore, he *needed to* spend time with his wife, and when the telephone rang he *had to* answer it. A person who thinks in absolutes does not easily tolerate any complicating factors. When things don't go as planned, frustration and anger are inevitable. So also is the probability of entering into conflicts with family members.

John provides another example. John was a newly called counselor in his ward bishopric. One particular Saturday was like many others. There was a car-wash activity for the youth, a wedding in a family he home taught, as well as a number of priorities to be taken care of at home with his family. John thought about all of these activities in terms of "have to." "I have to be at the car wash." "No way can I miss the wedding." "The family activities are a must." As a result, John had no choice. He had to do it all.

By seeing no choice, John got tense and became irritable on the Saturday in question. As is often the case, he controlled his irritability in his relationships outside the home, but he wasn't as good at hiding it from his family. They took the brunt of his anger, which was exactly the last thing that John wanted. Ironically, in this case, unwanted anger resulted from frustration over too many good things to do. Again, a concept from the Lord's marriage manual is helpful: "And see that all these things are done in wisdom and order; for it is not requisite that a man should run faster than he has strength. And again, it is expedient that he should be diligent, that thereby he might win the prize; therefore, all things must be done in order" (Mosiah 4:27). We apparently *do* have a choice as we pick and choose between the many demands on our time.

IT DOESN'T REALLY MATTER

As often as not, eliminating or reducing anger boils down to deciding that something we are agitated over just doesn't matter. The principle involved may matter, and important issues may be involved, but we must decide that the frustration doesn't matter to us, at least not enough to get upset about it. In spite of his best effort, the bishop's counselor in the previous example couldn't do everything that he would have liked on that particular Saturday. To find peace within himself he therefore had to *decide* that it didn't matter that some important things would not get done. The things themselves mattered, but the fact that he wasn't able to get to everything did not.

The dad who was angry at interruptions as he worked on a project had to *decide* that each interruption didn't matter. (Incidentally, his concentration was interrupted much more by his anger than by the little time it took to deal with the family interruptions.) To avoid becoming angry herself, his wife had to *decide* that it didn't matter that her husband was rude and inconsiderate when she tried to speak to him. Rude and inconsiderate behavior does matter. But when it involves the behavior of someone else, it's important that we take it in stride and not let it affect us in a negative way.

Therein lies an important rule as to whether or not we should let something matter. If the issue is beyond our control, it need not matter to us personally. We can care about it, pray about it, and do what is reasonable to resolve the problem. But it does no good to let it matter so much that we become personally upset about it. It's also appropriate to let it not matter when the issue isn't that important in the eternal scheme of things. As described below, much of what we get upset about may not matter at all in the long run.

WILL I CARE ABOUT IT FIFTY YEARS FROM NOW?

Asking this question can sometimes help convince us to not let something matter too much. Most things that are upsetting at the time have no long-term implications unless we react to them in a destructive way. An incident on the freeway, for instance, will soon be forgotten unless we chase after an offending driver and cause an accident in the process. Incidents in our families, no matter how painful at the time, might also look very different given the passage of time. A story I enjoy in this regard has to do with a woman and an old hat that her husband insisted on wearing. It was embarrassing to her when he wore the soiled and wrinkled hat in public, and she spent a lot of energy being angry about it. One day her husband died unexpectedly of a massive heart attack.

After his death, one of her most prized possessions was that same ugly old hat.

ANGER CONTROL AND OTHER VIRTUES

The examples given in the last two chapters illustrate the relationship between forgiveness and controlling anger. The decision to not let an offense matter, which is a key to controlling anger, is also one of the root issues in granting forgiveness. Forgiving, among other things, means releasing anger. Conversely, the presence of anger is proof that our willingness to forgive is not complete. As described below, humility also plays a part in avoiding and controlling anger. It's difficult to decide that something doesn't matter if our pride gets in the way and whatever *it* is becomes "a matter of principle."

CHAPTER THREE

BE HUMBLE

Yea, all of you be subject one to another,
and be clothed with humility: for God
resisteth the proud, and giveth grace to
the humble.

1 PETER 5:5

Pride rears its ugly head in our family relationships in any number of ways. It's there when we refuse to forgive another, or when we fail to control anger. It's represented by a wife unwilling to accept reasonable and well-motivated advice from her husband. It's also involved when a husband demands that his advice be followed and tries to *rule* rather than *lead* in the home. Pride is at work when parents refuse to admit mistakes or when children refuse to heed counsel.

As with other failures of virtue, it is often easy to see the problem in others but hard to see it in our-selves. Those who complain the loudest about their stubborn, pig-headed spouse are usually just a trifle stubborn and pig-headed themselves. As someone has pointed out, conceit is the strangest disease in the world. It makes everyone sick but the one who has it! When we are so afflicted, it's very difficult to admit that maybe, just maybe, the other person might be right.

YOU MIGHT BE RIGHT!

As novel as it sounds, we might not be right, even about an issue we feel pretty certain about. As a young missionary in the Eastern Canadian Mission a number of years ago, I and my companion had the responsibility of driving a visiting General Authority from the mission home in central Toronto to a missionary meeting. At the time there were two chapels in Toronto, each located on opposite ends of the city, with the mission home in the middle. I was absolutely certain that the meeting was to be held in the stake center on the west side of town. After a thirty-minute drive, with the General Authority seated in the backseat, it became obvious that I was wrong. We then had to turn around and retrace our steps in rush hour traffic. It took another hour to get to the right chapel, which made us all quite late for the meeting, but gave the General Authority a wonderful opportunity to lecture us on the merits of both being organized and being humble. Point taken!

Since it's always possible that we might be wrong, it does little harm to admit it. In fact, I believe there is great magic in the words "You might be right!" Words alone don't mean much if the attitude isn't there, but how refreshing it is to deal with someone who always gives others the benefit of the doubt—someone who refuses to insist on being right all the time. We certainly want to be that kind of person in our marriages and families.

When differences of opinion arise in family relationships, which they tend to do with regularity, I believe it's helpful to preface the expression of our opinion with the magic words "You might be right" or "Maybe so." Say my wife and I are driving someplace we haven't been, and we come to a decision point about directions. My wife might say, with perhaps more conviction than her sense of geography merits, "We need to turn left." Assume I am convinced that we need to turn right. What are my options?

I might remind my wife of previous times when she has been confused about directions and berate her for presuming to tell me where to go. But in doing so, I would surely offend her and hurt her feelings. Besides, wisdom ought to dictate that she might be correct, in spite of how certain I feel to the contrary.

Another option might seem to be a little wiser, but it really isn't. I could turn left (following her suggestion) but grouse about it. I could insist that it is probably the wrong way, complain about her back-seat driving, and so forth. By following this course, I would put a strain on our relationship and continue to offend her, not to mention set myself up for embarrassment should she turn out to be right.

A third option would be to happily turn left. I might do so in humility, knowing that she could be right, or I could do so simply in the interest of honoring her suggestion. Either way I would avoid doing damage to the relationship by being proud and stubborn. Either way I would be building our relationship rather than tearing it down. And if she turns out to be wrong, hopefully I could avoid saying, "I told you so." Even if a wrong turn makes us late, what is more important, the objective of our drive or nurturing our relationship?

A fourth option would work equally well. I might turn right (my choice) but use the magic words. It would go something like: "You might be right, but I'm pretty sure we need to turn this way. Let's go for a bit and check it out." I wouldn't be following her advice, but I would be conceding that she might be right. I would also avoid criticizing her idea or suggesting she doesn't know what she's talking about. In other words, I would do what I think is best without offending my partner.

While on this subject, may I mention that I might also get points for humility by stopping to ask for directions. For some reason (could it be pride?), asking for directions is something that most men find difficult to do.

I COULD BE WRONG!

Differences in opinion over small issues, such as directions or statements of fact, result in a surprising number of arguments in relationships. Adopting the "You might be right" attitude will help you avoid the nontrivial pain produced by arguments over trivial issues. But differences of opinion often arise over important issues—issues where it is difficult to compromise or to give the other the benefit of the doubt. Child rearing practices are an example.

It's not uncommon in a family for one parent to be stricter than the other with regard to disciplining children. Differences of opinion in this arena often cause conflict between parents. Let's say Dad believes in running a very tight ship and frequently gets upset with his wife for "letting the kids get away with murder." For her part, suppose Mom believes Dad is too strict and that his approach harms the children and creates tension in the home.

Since the welfare of the children and peace in the

home are of primary concern to both parents, this is a difficult conflict to resolve. But who is correct? Experts line up on both sides of the issue. If the parents were to seek help from any two counselors, they would probably get contradictory advice, depending on the value base of the individual counselors consulted. The fact is, Dad could be wrong in spite of being convinced that his approach is best. At the same time, Mom could be wrong regardless of her heartfelt opinion. To confuse the issue even more, they could both be right in the sense that what works best for Dad may not work best for Mom.

Exercising humility, as it is defined in God's marriage manual, can help resolve potential conflict in a situation such as this. In my experience, the most important issue isn't the style of discipline adopted in a family. It isn't even whether Dad and Mom agree with one another on how they discipline. The critical issue is whether or not Mom and Dad support each other in their individual efforts to discipline their children.

If humility were practiced in the example cited, Dad would discipline his way, but he would not criticize his wife or interfere with her more permissive approach when she disciplined or failed to discipline. Dad would also be open to learning from his wife and changing his approach somewhat if necessary. At the same time, Mom would discipline her way, but she would not criticize her husband or interfere with his more strict style. She, too, would be willing to learn from her husband and modify her approach where needed.

Children quickly learn how to take advantage of a situation in which one parent is more lenient than the other, but family solidarity and effective child rearing do not necessarily need to be compromised. Naturally an exception to this rule would be in incidents of blatant child abuse; but happily, those incidents are relatively rare. A significant problem is inevitable only when parents fight each other over their disagreement and undermine each other's efforts.

Unfortunately, most of us are familiar with situations where parents do fight over this issue. Mom makes a discipline decision, but then when the child complains to Dad, he modifies it or refuses to follow through on the discipline. Or conversely, it's Dad who lays down the law, but then Mom undermines it. Resulting arguments about discipline, often occurring within the hearing of children, are all too common. Again, practicing humility, which means allowing your partner to discipline his or her way without interference or attack from you, eliminates this destructive practice in families.

HUMILITY AND COURTESY

The pain caused by disagreements, even serious ones, is avoided when humility enters the equation. Another benefit of humility is that it engenders courteous behavior in our marriages and families. It allows a couple to follow Paul's advice: "Let the husband render unto the wife due benevolence: and likewise also the wife unto the husband" (1 Corinthians 7:3). Paul's instruction is a subset of the more general and quite famous rule taught by the Savior: "Therefore all things whatsoever ye would that men should do to you, do ye even so to them: for this is the law and the prophets" (Matthew 7:12).

Being humble and having respect for each other is what enables us to live the Golden Rule in our families. Humility derives from recognizing that we aren't perfect and that we are totally and universally dependent on the Lord. To be humble is to also recognize that we are all children of the same God and that all of us are of infinite value and worth to Him. With this perspective, we will naturally treat our spouse, or anyone else for that matter, with respect.

Imagine that you are in the presence of someone for whom you have great respect—the prophet, for example. You would pay him the courtesy of listening carefully to what he has to say because you value his opinion. You might even actively seek his counsel on various issues if the opportunity presented itself. You certainly wouldn't think to be critical of him, and you would look for ways to make him comfortable. You would probably open the door for him, make certain he is seated comfortably, and perhaps offer refreshments. You would be most comfortable if you knew he was comfortable. Efforts to make him so would be gladly made without hesitation.

If you truly respect your spouse, you will be equally solicitous of his or her comfort. You will listen to and take pleasure in finding ways to serve your partner. If you are a man, you might even make sure that the toilet seat is lowered after use. If you are a woman who sees no use for football, you might even sit down and watch a game with your husband. Having respect means you honor your commitments to each other. If you promise to be home at a certain time, you are. If you promise to complete a chore, you do so. You will also recognize and avoid pushing any hot buttons that your spouse might have.

We all have hot buttons. My wife very much enjoys physical contact, but she hates to be poked, even in a teasing way. I enjoy tickling and poking, but out of respect for my wife, that's something I try to avoid doing. I hate messy countertops. I can stand for drawers to be messy, but things need to be put out of sight. This is not a priority for my wife, but out of respect for me, she keeps things picked up. We certainly aren't perfect in our treatment of each other, but over the years we have learned that courteous behavior enhances the overall quality of our relationship. We have also learned that our willingness to treat each other courteously corresponds to the degree of humility we feel at the moment.

HUMILITY AND CONFESSION

Being humble also enables us to readily admit our mistakes. To be willing to confess our faults and shortcomings is another of the instructions found in God's marriage manual. James taught, "Confess your faults one to another" (James 5:16). Occasionally a person commits a sin which, because of its magnitude, must be confessed to those offended, and also to Church and civil authorities. Confessing a serious sin, especially voluntarily, before it is discovered, requires a great deal of humility. Humility also makes it possible to confront and resolve lesser offenses, such as inevitably occur in intimate relationships.

We may, for instance, inadvertently or even purposefully push one of those hot buttons just mentioned. Suppose I come home tired and irritable to an untidy house. Things will work best if I can overlook the problem, as suggested in previous chapters. But since it's one of my hot buttons and since I'm tired and irritable anyway, it's going to be a struggle to handle the situation properly. The struggle will be made much easier if my wife "confesses." All she has to say is, "I'm sorry the house is a mess. I'll get to it when I can." That sincere statement is enough to give me the extra something I need to let go of the problem emotionally and make it a nonissue.

As helpful as this simple comment would be, it can't be offered without humility on my wife's part. This is true in part because she really hasn't done anything wrong. It's my hot button (hang-up) that is involved. The house is messy because she has been involved in other things, she doesn't feel well, or she simply hasn't cared about it at that moment. None of which is a sin. But here she is apologizing anyway. That takes humility.

It's hard to admit a mistake when it's a mistake only in the eyes of the person to whom we apologize. And it's hard to admit mistakes in general because doing so is embarrassing. Acknowledging a mistake is to make a tacit admission that we aren't perfect. But to frankly admit a mistake is infinitely better than to mount a prideful counterattack or attempt to place the blame on something or someone else. To my wife's credit she never does this, but on the day of the messy house she could have pointed out how unreasonable my demands were and how insensitive I was. She would be correct, but making a comment of that kind would have made for an interesting evening at home.

Again, she avoids doing so, but my wife might also make excuses, claiming this or that as the reason for the messy house. We all know those who persist in blaming something or someone for every negative thing in their life. These folks are not able to grow, and it isn't easy to relate to them. Making excuses also opens up an opportunity for unnecessary debate. If such a husband says he was too busy to get to a promised chore, such a wife's tendency is to debate how true that is. "Well, you had plenty of time to read the newspaper!" To which comment the husband will have a rejoinder. Such debate can quickly escalate into an argument, whereas a humble "I'm sorry" defuses any further animosity.

HUMILITY AND SERVICE

It has already been pointed out that humility engenders respect, which in turn fosters a desire to be of service. The requirement to serve one another is another of the basic tenets found in the Lord's marriage manual (for example, see Matthew 20:25-27 and Matthew 25:34-40). The good news is that we naturally want to help and make comfortable those we respect. There are limits, however, on the kind of service a proud individual will offer.

Numbers in this category are decreasing, but there are still men out there who would never do housework. No matter how much their spouse might appreciate such help, some husbands feel it's simply beneath them to clean toilets. There are women, again the numbers are shrinking, who would never think of doing yard work or working on cars. They refuse, not because they can't for some reason, but because they wouldn't feel right about it. They might be reluctant simply because they think, "That's his (her) job!" Or perhaps they think it's not fair, given their many other responsibilities, to be expected to do such work.

If we are truly humble, we will do what's necessary to get the job done in our families. Both Mom and Dad change the dirty diapers, and both Mom and Dad make calls to set up appointments. No job is beneath either one. They each do whatever is required. Interestingly, some who refuse to do unpleasant tasks don't recognize that their behavior is prideful. They might even represent their reluctance as an evidence of humility: "I don't do that because I'm no good at it. My wife/husband does it so much better." A careful look reveals that this is still pride-based behavior. In some cases, the individual is not humble enough to do something poorly in an effort to get better at it. In others, claiming a lower skill level is just a convenient excuse to avoid doing what they believe to be a demeaning task.

If we would be humble, we would also be willing to serve one another, even when we believe our partner doesn't deserve it. There are times when it is hard to respect a person based on his or her current behavior. As an example, I'm thinking of a husband who is demanding and puts his wife down in public. His poor treatment of his wife is in no way defensible, and he must change his behavior if they are to have a good marriage. But in spite of how the wife is treated, she is still obligated to treat her husband well. This requirement comes directly from the Lord, "But I say unto you, That ye resist not evil: but whosoever shall smite thee on the right cheek, turn to him the other also. And if any man will sue thee at the law, and take away thy coat, let him have thy cloke also. And whosoever shall compel thee to go a mile, go with him twain" (Matthew 5:39-41).

As a side note, the Lord's direction to turn the other cheek does not mean that a victim of spousal abuse must submit to repeated brutality. Surely the Lord does not expect woman (or man, for that matter) to endure such treatment. But in the case of what might be termed "garden variety" mistreatment—

things such as a spouse being insensitive to our needs, failing to help us when we need and deserve it, and making critical comments—we need to be patient and forgiving. This is true for any and all of at least a half dozen reasons: (1) We want to be a good person, and that's what a good person does. (2) That way, we are at least doing our part to make the relationship work. (3) We can feel good about ourselves if we do the right thing, even if our partner or child does not. (4) Our good example might help the other change. (5) Our good example can positively influence children or other observers. (6) Trying to get even, or trying to fight fire with fire, will make everything worse. There are always good reasons for following the Lord's directions, even if those reasons are not always immediately evident to us.

How is it possible to willingly do nice things for an undeserving spouse or child? The answer lies in our being truly humble. And how do we gain such humility? By remembering that we, ourselves, are fallible and weak and completely dependent on the Lord for the remission of our own sins. Except for His grace, none of us has any hope. It helps too, to remind ourselves that those who offend us are still children of God, with infinite potential, and that He loves them. By thinking of the members of our family, even those who offend us, in these terms, we can learn to love and serve them. Humility makes it possible.

HUMILITY AND UNSOLICITED ADVICE

While on the subject of service in marriage, it's probably worth noting that trying to help can sometimes be overdone. This is especially true if the help we are offering takes the form of giving advice. In many situations, unsolicited advice ends up sounding like criticism. Or if not heard as criticism, it's at least confusing and frustrating when we are given unwanted suggestions. Backseat driving is a classic example. Yes, it may be because we aren't humble enough, but who among us doesn't get at least a little upset if someone makes comments about our driving? On the other side of it, why do some spouses insist on giving directions that they know aren't appreciated? Couldn't that also be pride at work? They are sure they know what's best (pride at work), and they feel obligated to get their spouse to see the light (pride again).

Unsolicited advice is particularly obnoxious when offered in stressful situations. The water pipe under the sink just broke. The car has broken down on the way to an important meeting. We have a troubling situation to deal with at work or at church. Our calendar is hopelessly clogged with important assignments. When we are struggling to deal with stressful situations such as these, the last thing we may feel we need is a spouse giving us directions, no matter how well-motivated or correct that counsel might be. Listening, offering help, *following* directions, and showing concern can be helpful. *Giving* directions and advice usually is not. It's often best to back off and let the responsible partner handle the situation without our interference (help).

There are also cases where spouses are so intent on helping their partner that their efforts are counterproductive. An example of this is a spouse who has the habit of finishing sentences for his or her partner when the partner takes a little too long to complete a thought. Another is the martyr who always goes along with a spouse's wishes, but then is resentful of how "selfish" his or her partner is.

IT'S NOT EASY, BUT IT'S WORTH IT.

Though it is a necessary thing in a family, it is not easy to always practice humility. It is especially difficult when we understand that having a humble attitude is as important as behaving humbly. It's one thing for the wife in a previous example to continue to do nice things for her undeserving husband, and quite another thing to do so with a good attitude. Behaving humbly is important for its own sake, but it clearly works better when our heart and mind are right too. Otherwise we stress ourselves unnecessarily. It's psychologically painful to act in a way that contradicts our values. We also undermine the good we might do if we reveal our resentment or give some indication that the service is being reluctantly given. Service that looks to the recipient as though it is grudgingly given is usually resented. Or it may be interpreted as a manipulative device.

Acquiring the degree of humility Christ seems to require of us will be a lifelong pursuit for most of us. It is a pursuit that takes contemplation, prayer, and effort over time. We need to remind ourselves frequently that we might not be right in various situations and that we are totally dependent on the Lord. Is the kind of effort required worth it? You bet! We know it is because of the witness of those who have achieved this goal—preeminent among them being the Savior Himself, who performed the ultimate act of humility when, in the Garden and on the cross, He sacrificed Himself for all of us.

CHAPTER FOUR

AVOID COVETING

———

Thou shalt not covet thy neighbour's house, thou shalt not covet thy neighbour's wife, nor his manservant, nor his maidservant, nor his ox, nor his ass, nor any thing that is thy neighbour's.

EXODUS 20:17

This is the tenth and last, but certainly not the least, of the Ten Commandments. Throughout history, the ungodly pursuit of wealth and power has lain at the root of most of the world's misery. Both current events and history are replete with descriptions of megalomaniacs who have subjugated and plundered their countrymen and neighbors through murder and oppression. Religious tyrants, crime lords, and syndicates and just plain ordinary thieves, liars, and murderers round out the list of those driven by an uncontrolled and ungodly desire to possess something, i.e., those who covet.

As the following examples indicate, coveting also wreaks havoc in our marriages and families.

COVETING ATTENTION

Hank was painfully aware that his marriage was not fulfilling, but he had no idea that plain, old-fashioned coveting was at the root of his problem. In fact, Hank was convinced that the problem in his marriage was his wife's fault. In his opinion, she simply failed to give him the degree of love that he needed. She wasn't as sexually aggressive as he wanted her to be. When he was feeling amorous, she was too often preoccupied with needs of the children or some other concern. She also frequently busied herself with duties outside the home, in the community and at church. It was obvious to Hank that he wasn't the most important element in his wife's life, and there were times when she didn't even seem to like him that much.

In essence, Hank coveted time and attention from his wife. He was jealous when she focused on the children or when she served others in need. Frequently his thought was, "Why can't she treat *me* that nicely?" He coveted the warmth and support he saw other wives giving their husbands. "Why can't my wife show *me* that kind of affection?" He coveted the old days prior to marriage when he was clearly the center of his future wife's life. "Why can't she love me the way she used to?"

Coveting is a narcissistic sin. It's one that empha-
sizes *me*. Hank was much more focused on what he
wanted to get from his wife than on what he was giving to her. When challenged on the point, he was
quick to defend himself by reciting a long list of his
efforts to give of himself. And in fact he had and did
give a lot. But the problem was in his focus. He was
focused too much on what he was or was not receiv-
ing in his marriage. And as is always the case in such
relationships, his scorekeeping wasn't accurate. He
often overlooked, misjudged, or discounted efforts by
his wife to express love and support. And as is also
typical, Hank's own giving was often conditional. He
frequently gave, to make a point or to manipulate or
to bargain.

Naturally, Hank wanted from his marriage what
we all want—to feel loved and accepted. But this
desire, which is normal and good, can sometimes get
out of hand and turn into coveting. We cross over the
line when the compulsion to obtain something
(warmth, approval, sex, or whatever) becomes so
important to us that we can't be content without it.
We are over the edge if that desire begins to dominate
our thinking and dictate our moods, and we are guilty
of coveting when we need that something so badly
that we use compulsion to get it.

Perhaps Hank's wife really ought to focus on him

more, and he has a right to voice his desire and to do whatever is reasonable to get her to see his point. But, if getting her to dote on him continues to be a compulsion with him, his coveting her attention will end up destroying his peace of mind and poisoning their relationship.

Whatever his wife does, the best thing Hank can do for himself and his marriage is to focus on being the best person he can be. Period! The issue then isn't "Does my wife love me?" or "How *much* does she love me;" but rather, "Am I lovable?" or "How lovable am I?" If Hank can honestly feel good about his treatment of his wife, and if he is kind and forgiving and all those good things, then he can feel good about himself and be happy in his life, whether or not he gets everything he feels he ought to from his wife.

This was actually the strategy Hank's wife followed with good success. She was hurt over the years by Hank's basic criticism that she was a disappointment as a wife. She tried her best to live up to his expectations, but was generally frustrated. Her best efforts never seemed to be sufficient. At one point she decided that enough was enough. She came to the conclusion: "I can't please him, so I'm not going to try. I'm going to continue to treat him well because it's the right thing to do, but I'm not going to let Hank's criticisms of me determine how I live my life or how I feel about myself."

Hank's wife decided to use God's standard, not Hank's, to evaluate how well she was doing in her life. By trusting Hank's opinions, she was in a sense trusting "in the arm of flesh"—something we have been warned against doing in God's marriage manual (see D&C 1:19). Of course, we need to be open to learn about ourselves from our spouse, as discussed in the previous chapter, but moral judgments need to be based on gospel principles, not the opinions of others.

As Hank's case illustrates, coveting attention causes pain, both for the one who covets, and for his or her spouse. It's almost as devastating as coveting a relationship outside of marriage.

COVETING ANOTHER'S SPOUSE

Many divorces and a great deal of pain in families can be traced to coveting another relationship. Elder Spencer W. Kimball made this point convincingly:

"There are those who look with longing eyes, who want and desire and crave these romantic associations. So to desire to possess, to inordinately want and yearn for such, is to covet, and the Lord in powerful terms condemns it: 'And again, I command thee that thou shalt not covet thy neighbor's wife; nor seek thy neighbor's life' (D&C 19:25).

"How powerful! The seventh and tenth commandments are interwoven into one great command, which is awesome in its warning. To covet that which belongs to another is sin, and that sin begins when hearts begin to entertain a glamorous interest in anyone else. There are many tragedies affecting spouses, children, and loved ones. Even though these 'affairs' begin near-innocently, like an octopus the tentacles move gradually to strangle.

"When dates or dinners or rides or other contacts begin, the abyss of tragedy opens wide its mouth. And, it has reached deep iniquity when physical contacts of any nature have been indulged in. Man's desire is fed and nurtured by [his] food-thoughts" (in Conference Report, October 1962, 58–59).

I assume that "food-thoughts," as Elder Kimball referred to them, are perceptions, observations, and private thoughts that lead to coveting. Mary, unfortunately, became attracted to her manager at work. Unlike her husband, Tom was so easy to talk to. Mary and he frequently stayed late at the office to "discuss work." They both really enjoyed these times, and being together became a priority for both of them. On the other hand, Mary's conversations with her husband were difficult. He was very quiet and hard to talk to, and he often got defensive and became critical. This was not so with her manager. Mary could talk to Tom about anything for hours, and enjoyed doing so.

Unlike her husband, Tom seemed to genuinely care for her. He was solicitous and courteous. It was obvious that he appreciated her work. He admired her intellect, he enjoyed her personality, and he found Mary to be physically attractive. It seemed as though everything she was missing in her relationship with her husband was available in the relationship she had with her manager.

What "food-thoughts" did Mary entertain? Regarding her manager, she thought, "I'm important to him." "He thinks I'm wonderful." "He makes me happy." "Life's too short to be unhappy." "I could be happy forever with him." "We are truly soul mates." Regarding her husband, she thought, "He doesn't really care for me." "He doesn't respect me." "He makes me miserable." "Life's too short to be miserable all the time." "I'll never be happy as long as I'm with him." "I should never have married him." Notice that her thoughts were not overtly sexual, which Mary would have considered to be inappropriate. But by fixating on Tom and continually making comparisons between him and her husband, she entertained the rationalizations that led inevitably to an illicit sexual relationship, thus illustrating the subtle process that leads to adultery.

Thinking as she did, it's not hard to imagine the outcome. Mary's belief that her manager made her happy and her husband made her miserable, fueled by constant "food-thoughts" as suggested above, created an overwhelming desire in Mary to leave her husband and to be with her manager. Her covetous thoughts overpowered her commitment to her marriage and her values. Ironically, she even reached the point where she felt guilty being with her husband and felt more comfortable in what by then had become an adulterous relationship. The total cost of her coveting may not be known until after this life, but it already includes the breakup of two families and an enormous emotional upheaval in the lives of everyone involved.

Some might argue that Mary's problem wasn't the thoughts she entertained and the choices she made, but rather the fact that her manager treated her well and her husband did not. The world is full of people who would say that life is too short to be unhappy and that Mary would be a fool to pass up a chance to improve her life. There are at least three points that should be considered by those who are tempted to think this way.

ILLUSIONS

First, there is always a real question about whether life will actually improve by changing partners. Mary found something in the relationship she had with her manager that was lacking in her marriage, but there is no guarantee that such advantages would continue once real life sets in. Mr. Wonderful can quickly turn into Mr. Ordinary or even Mr. Disaster. Complicated and inevitable emotional issues involving children, friends, and extended family members can also be very disruptive to a peaceful and fulfilling life.

SHORTSIGHTEDNESS

Second, those who rationalize by saying, "Life is too short" are obviously thinking only about mortal life. Those who focus too much on finding happiness in this life may be forgetting the fact that life continues. It's most shortsighted to sell one's birthright for a pottage of lentils (see Genesis 25:29–34), which is what happens whenever we make decisions that provide momentary pleasure, but at the expense of our long-term welfare. Remember, the piper must be paid.

RIPPLE EFFECT

Lastly, it should be remembered that an illicit affair adversely affects a marriage on at least two levels. First, the affair inevitably causes subtle or not so subtle behavioral changes in the adulterous partner, which changes lead to communication problems and other difficulties in the primary relationship. Second, an affair certainly reinforces and may even create a perception that one's marriage is flawed, probably as a result of the need to justify the adultery. History is reconstructed, as in, "I never loved him/her." A dissatisfied spouse may also exaggerate his or her frustration, as in "I can't talk to him about anything." In other words, once an individual covets another relationship, the very fact of coveting weakens the existing marriage, both in perception and in reality.

The Lord's marriage manual says: "For this cause shall a man leave father and mother, and shall cleave to his wife: and they twain shall be one flesh. Wherefore they are no more twain, but one flesh. What therefore God hath joined together, let not man put asunder" (Matthew 19:5-6). The word *cleave* means "to stick," and it suggests action on everyone's part. In other words, we must think and do things that promote union. We must avoid thinking and doing things that lead to disunion.

In another place the Lord says, "But I say unto you, That whosoever looketh on a woman to lust after her hath committed adultery with her already in his heart" (Matthew 5:28). This, I believe, is a reminder of how insidious the process is that leads people to commit adultery. The sin may originate in a thought that is not even sexual and therefore seems innocuous. Then the thought leads to behavior that is mostly innocent and can be easily rationalized. Finally, we have gone too far.

As the Lord Himself, President Kimball, and other prophets have suggested, we make a dangerous mistake when we allow ourselves to covet another relationship. Those who do so should count the cost. They need to ask themselves, "What am I willing to pay for this?" Infidelity is likely to cost way more than it can possibly be worth. It also helps to recognize that even a compelling and overpowering desire to be with someone will disappear over time *if the desire is not fed*. And, as described previously, the desire to possess another relationship is fed by "food-thoughts," i.e., the things we *choose* to think about. Finally, a simple rule works perfectly in guaranteeing that a married person will never commit adultery. Don't spend time alone with anyone of the opposite sex, no matter how innocent that time together might seem at the moment. Just don't do it, *ever*, and the chances of committing adultery are zero. Remember, many a moth has thought it harmless to dance around the flame, but has paid the ultimate price for miscalculating the danger.

MISCELLANEOUS COVETING

The foregoing examples are of what happens when we covet nonmaterial things such as attention or the affections of someone else's spouse. Of course, regular old coveting of *things* can also be destructive. One husband I know brought (bought) his family to the brink of financial ruin because he simply had to have a new, expensive car on a regular basis. He "needed" to live in a home that stretched the family budget to the point of breaking. His clothes had to be the best quality, and his family had to give the appearance of financial success and prosperity.

It's not difficult to imagine the strain the pursuit of such "needs" put on his family. He worked inordinately long hours and was physically and emotionally exhausted when he returned home. He was unable to give his family the time and attention they needed from him. His wife was forced to work outside the home, which meant that she too was unable to adequately meet the needs of their family. Tension created by financial worries permeated the marriage and caused relentless personal stress for both husband and wife. All of these problems were exacerbated by the fact that the wife didn't agree with her husband's spending priorities. Many heated discussions occurred over spending decisions.

It was clear to his wife, but interestingly, the husband in this situation did not realize that he was coveting. He had convinced himself that his spending priorities were not only justified, they were mandated. In his work he marketed investment opportunities. He felt certain that in order to be successful he had to present the appearance of financial success. He had convinced himself that he didn't really need, or even want all of these things for himself. They were simply a business necessity—a legitimate business expense.

In fact, it's very likely that he could have been successful in his work even if he had spent much less on appearances. He probably didn't need the Mercedes, and the big house didn't help any since he didn't see clients at home. Presenting a nice physical appearance was important, but wearing designer clothes probably was not. Even if he were right, and an expensive lifestyle was necessary to be successful in his line of work, he didn't need to stay in that line of work. Any way it's analyzed, the truth is that he simply didn't need the luxuries that he thought he did.

This tendency to redefine a situation to justify an

unhealthy desire for something as a "need" is fairly
typical. Few people who are guilty of coveting ever recognize it as such or easily face up to the fact. Usually
there is a justification: "It's way too expensive, but I
need this dress to make me feel better." "We can't
really afford this house, but we need the room." "This
car is too expensive, but I need reliable transporta-
tion." "We don't really have enough money to pur-
chase cable TV, but it's our only form of recreation."
The kinds of things we covet are often not sinful in
themselves, but an inordinate desire to have them is.
By definition, a "need" is inordinate if it leads to purchases we can't afford and/or if we are unable to be
happy without the item.

The negative impact of coveting is usually felt
most acutely in our family relationships. As Jesus
taught: "Take heed, and beware of covetousness: for a
man's life consisteth not in the abundance of the
things which he possesseth. And he spake a parable
unto them, saying, The ground of a certain rich man
brought forth plentifully: And he thought within himself, saying, What shall I do, because I have no room
where to bestow my fruits? And he said, this will I do:
I will pull down my barns, and build greater; and
there will I bestow all my fruits and my goods. And I
will say to my soul, Soul, thou hast much goods laid
up for many years; take thine ease, eat, drink, and be

merry. But God said unto him, Thou fool, this night thy soul shall be required of thee: then whose shall those things be, which thou hast provided? So is he that layeth up treasure for himself, and is not rich toward God" (Luke 12:15–21).

We covet when our focus is on obtaining things of the world at the expense of keeping the commandments of God. We are coveting whenever we demand or require something in this world in order to be happy—be that new clothes, a car, acceptance, agreement, or whatever. As suggested earlier, this might even apply in our pursuit of a basically righteous goal. For example, having a perfect family may be so important to us that we would manipulate, coerce, or lie (act unrighteously) in an effort to get family members to conform.

Criticism and judgment of those we love usually result from an ill-advised attempt to get family members to change to become who or what we need them to be, and being covetous of a righteous goal often leads us to unrighteously judge one another, as described in the next chapter.

CHAPTER FIVE

AVOID JUDGING

———

*Judge not, that ye be not judged. For with
what judgment ye judge, ye shall be
judged: and with what measure ye mete, it
shall be measured to you again. And why
beholdest thou the mote that is in thy
brother's eye, but considerest not the beam
that is in thine own eye? Or how wilt thou
say to thy brother, Let me pull out the
mote out of thine eye; and, behold, a beam
is in thine own eye? Thou hypocrite, first
cast out the beam out of thine own eye;
and then shalt thou see clearly to cast out
the mote out of thy brother's eye.*

MATTHEW 7:1-5

One of the most common refrains in current marriage therapy is the doctrine that
we can't change our partners; all we can
do is change ourselves. As the above quote from the
New Testament suggests, this concept has been
around for a while. Its truth is self-evident, and
though most people readily agree with it, not too

many live by it. It's amusing to watch couples who come seeking marriage counseling give lip service to the concept in counseling sessions, while ignoring it in practice. They often say something such as: "I know I have to change myself. I know not all of our problems are his (her) fault, *but* . . ." and then they go on to harangue their partner and list in great detail the other's faults, usually becoming quite agitated if they are interrupted before completing their diatribe.

These are people who believe that the solution to the problems in their marriage is to get their partner into therapy. These are they who manipulate, demand, and coerce their partners into the bishop's and/or a marriage counselor's office. Their primary goal, apparently, is to get an authority figure on their side. "Maybe the bishop can talk some sense into him." These are folks who go on and on to their friends and anyone else who will listen about their spouse's faults, often after making the obligatory but insincere disclaimer, "I know I'm not perfect either . . ." In fact, they may be correct about their partner's failings. He or she may be guilty as charged; but their strategy for effecting change is wrong. As it reads in God's marriage manual, "Thou hypocrite, first cast out the beam out of thine own eye; and then shalt thou see clearly to cast out the mote out of thy brother's eye" (Matthew 7:5).

The counsel found in God's marriage manual, seconded by virtually all current marriage therapists, is that we should try to change ourselves, not our partners—for one primary reason—because that's the only way it works! We have power to change ourselves, but in spite of how often and how hard we try, we can't change others. This being true, someone might ask, What do you do if your spouse is unfaithful to you or is physically abusive? Such circumstances are on a short list of behaviors that may make living with a person untenable. These are things of such a serious nature that unless the abusive or unfaithful partner changes, the marriage is over. How can someone be nonjudgmental in that type of situation?

Some people have the notion that a truly non-judgmental person would stay in the marriage and be forgiving no matter what. The truth is that though God's marriage manual does require that we be forgiving, it does not necessarily stipulate that we must stay in such a marriage. As discussed at length in chapter seven, divorce is rarely an acceptable option, and there are very few justifiable reasons to end a marriage. But those reasons do exist.

A victim of infidelity, or other behaviors on this short list of justifiable reasons, can make very clear what the limits are that he or she will tolerate in his or her partner's behavior. The partner then has a choice of going forward, having had fair warning of what will happen if he or she repeats the offensive behavior. This is a very different approach from resorting to name-calling, criticizing, and using constant put-downs, in an effort to shame, coerce, or manipulate the spouse into changing.

In this regard, it helps to recognize the difference between righteous and unrighteous judgment. Under inspiration, Joseph Smith made an important correction to Matthew 7:1 quoted above. As corrected, the Lord's instruction is to "Judge not *unrighteously,* that ye be not judged: but judge *righteous* judgment" (JST, Matthew 7:2; emphasis added). Judging righteously means making *correct* judgments, which is not easy to do, especially when we are evaluating the values and behaviors of another person. But that is what we must do. We also need to make judgments about what course of action we will take in response to the mistakes of others. This too can be done in righteousness. One thing we must avoid is engaging in the negative, critical carping typically found in so many marriages.

CRITICIZING THE LITTLE THINGS

If it is counterproductive and destructive to criticize (exercise unrighteous judgment) while trying to help our partner repent of major sins, it is equally so with regard to more routine and mundane things. George, for example, was constantly on his wife's case, criticizing virtually everything she did. He criticized her for wearing the blue dress when the red dress was obviously so much more attractive on her. He criticized her for taking a second helping at the dinner table. He complained about the way she disciplined the children, pointing out that she was "weak" and "inconsistent" and that she was letting the kids run all over her.

In a mistaken belief that his critical comments would be less offensive and have a greater effect, George would sometimes combine a compliment with his put-downs. "You are extremely intelligent; I can't understand why you don't use your brain more." Or "I know you can cook well; why don't you take the time to do it right?" He would also justify making a critical comment because he was willing to include himself. "I know I've done stupid things like that myself, but . . ." Such a strategy did nothing to soften the blows and still had a devastating effect on his wife and on their relationship.

George also excused his destructive behavior on philosophical grounds. He felt justified in criticizing her because he had only his wife's best interests at heart. In his opinion, she really did look better in the red dress, and he was simply trying to help her make a good impression. She was overweight, and he knew she would feel better physically and emotionally if she were to trim down. She was at times overwrought by the kids, and he wanted to help her be more effective with them. There were times when he was just tired and irritable, and he realized that the critical outbursts he made at those times were just that—critical outbursts—but more often, he was only trying to help, so he couldn't understand why she would get so upset. In fact, that was another of her shortcomings. "You're just too sensitive; you're going to have to get a tougher skin," he would tell her.

To live comfortably with George, she would indeed need a tougher skin, as would anyone else for that matter. The fact that his criticism was well-motivated didn't make it any easier to bear. His constant reminders that she was not measuring up reinforced his wife's low opinion of herself and made her feel even less adequate as a marriage partner. It also made intimacy impossible. It's hard to warm up to someone who is always putting us down. It's hard to be close to someone from inside a defensive shell, which we have had to construct to protect us from constant attack.

George's wife wanted the marriage to work, but she ended up not liking her husband very much. Because he was so often critical of her, she avoided conversations with him. And, enjoying shared activities was usually a challenge. Likely as not,

George would say something negative, which would cast a pall over an otherwise fun outing. But the ultimate challenge was to maintain their sexual relationship. Based on her fear of George and her resentment of him, it was extremely difficult for her to share a bed, which gave George something else to criticize. He frequently complained that his wife was a "cold fish" with "obvious sexual hang-ups."

What is the solution to such a problem in a marriage? One solution would be for George to come to grips with his sins and repent. No matter how well meaning, his continuing to harp on his wife was a big mistake and needed to end. This would be possible only by his focusing on *his* problems in the marriage and not hers. And that would be possible only if he humbly recognized his own errors and made a sincere effort to change his behavior. In other words, he needs to follow the proven guidelines in God's marriage manual.

Unfortunately for George's wife, she could do little to get him to change. If in a judgmental way she were to try to get George to see the light and repent, she would be making the same mistake herself. And in fact, that was happening in the marriage. Her tactics were different, but in her own way she was trying to manipulate George. As suggested above, sexual intimacy for the couple was very difficult in its own right, but she used sexual withdrawal as a weapon to get

George to change. She also drew from her arsenal emotional outbursts and her own brand of name-calling. In their arguments, she would scream at George about what a tyrant he was and about how his constant criticism was evil. Of course, she was right in her assessment of her husband's behavior but quite wrong in the way she responded to his provocations.

A better strategy for George's wife would have been to approach the problem unilaterally, as suggested in God's marriage manual. Rather than focusing on her husband's behavior, which was beyond her control, she needed to focus on her own. She would need the Lord's help in this situation, but as described in earlier chapters, she could work on forgiving George and on eliminating the anger she felt toward him.

Coveting was also a problem as she imagined how much better marriage would be with someone else. That she could fix. She could work on getting rid of her judgmental attitude toward her husband and her subtle or not-so-subtle attempts to compel him to change. There was nothing wrong with her judgment that his actions were out of line. That was a righteous judgment. But there was something wrong with her judgment that *he* was out of line—an unrighteous judgment. She often thought of George as a failure as a human being and as a truly evil person. Some people are evil, but in this case, George was only misguided.

By following God's marriage manual, the wife would be able to confront George's criticism in a more effective way. She could clearly let him know how offensive his treatment of her was, without putting him down in the process. Ultimately, she could even get to where his criticism had little emotional effect on her. If she knew on a spiritual level that she was a good person and that the Lord generally approved of her, that would go a long way toward helping her maintain her self-confidence and peace of mind in spite of her husband's contrary opinions.

She could then react as she did whenever anyone criticized her religious beliefs. She had a relative who frequently put down her faith and belittled her membership in the Church. Those were uncomfortable encounters, but she was able to get past them without emotional damage because she was secure in her faith. It really didn't matter what this relative said—she knew in her heart that her faith was correct. Likewise, it would be possible for her to be confident that she is a good person and that her choices are appropriate, even if George didn't seem to agree.

Clearly, such a marriage will not reach its potential until both husband and wife get with the program. It is, in fact, a recipe for disaster when one of the partners remains judgmental and concentrates only on trying to manipulate his or her partner's behavior.

It doesn't solve the whole problem either if only one partner modifies his or her behavior, but working unilaterally can still make a difference. Example can have a powerful effect. Typically, when one partner begins to make a positive change, so then does the other. However, it's necessary to be patient (see chapter seven). Otherwise, we may grow weary and give up prematurely, thus creating a yo-yo effect in which one partner changes for a season but gets discouraged and reverts. Then the other begins working on their problems, but their two efforts don't coincide or overlap.

To succeed, we need to be patient, and we need to stay motivated. The goal in repenting should be to improve ourselves, not to improve our marriage, per se. We can't control whether we have a great marriage or not, but we can control whether we are a great person or not. We need to do the right thing because it is the right thing to do, not because it will change our partner. That way, the necessary patience becomes a given, and we end up doing our part to have a great marriage consistently, no matter what.

SO WHAT DOES IT MEAN TO BE CRITICAL?

George was similar to a lot of critical people. He had a hard time believing that he was too judgmental. Often it seemed to him that his wife would take offense where none was intended. And indeed she did. Because she was criticized so often, she was extra sensitive and just naturally jumped to negative conclusions. It's easy to misjudge another's intentions and assume criticism when it really isn't intended. Suppose your wife compliments a man you both know about how nicely he dresses. That wouldn't necessarily mean that she is being critical of your appearance. Or suppose she complains about not having enough time with you. That could be heard as a criticism of how you choose to spend your time, or she might simply be expressing a frustration for which she doesn't particularly blame you.

Marriage partners sometimes jump to the conclusion that their partner is attacking them when, in fact, that might not be the case. A reasonable (nonjudgmental) person will at least ask for clarification when it appears he or she is the object of criticism. "Are you saying that you don't think I dress well?" Or "Are you saying that you think I'm not trying hard enough to find time for you?" Asking a direct question can often clarify whether or not any criticism was intended. When asked directly to say what they mean, critics will often soften their statements, thus defusing the situation somewhat and, perhaps, providing the stimulus to a more productive discussion. This is not likely to happen if one jumps immediately on the defensive with a comment such as "Why are you always on my case about how I dress?" or "Don't you realize how much pressure I'm under at work?"

Whether criticism is taken as constructive or not depends ultimately on how we receive it. God's marriage manual teaches us that we need to be humble and willing to learn from others, as discussed in the previous chapter. By following this scriptural guideline, we can get past the tendency we have to resist suggestions made by others for our improvement, so that we can learn from those close to us. Sometimes the suggestion is without merit and can be discarded. In other instances, there really is something that we need to change about ourselves. One tip-off that the shoe might fit is how sensitive we are to the feedback. Criticism usually stings the most when we most deserve it!

Based on everything I have observed, it would be well if marriage partners would refrain from offering each other "constructive criticism." It is a rare spouse who can graciously accept a suggestion that he or she has performed poorly or has a deficiency that needs to be corrected—especially if the word *should* is used in the sentence. It doesn't matter what the truth might be. It doesn't matter how well intentioned the advice. Any time we presume to tell our spouse something he or she *should* do differently, the recommendation is almost certain to be poorly received.

So, is there a way to make critical comments and not have them be offensive? Well, in marriage, maybe not. But there are some ways the sender can hedge the bet. Here are a few pointers to consider:

1. Critical comments (those with the word *should* included or implied) ought to be kept to an absolute minimum. As suggested in chapter two, many things that concern us just don't matter that much.

2. We need to pick the right time to give negative feedback. That means avoiding times when we aren't at our emotional best and/or when it is clear our partner is not feeling up to hearing something negative. Remember that timing sometimes is everything!

3. Be polite about it. How suggestions for improvement are stated does make a difference. For instance, rather than make a *demand,* we can describe a personal *need.* That way we are asking for a favor. "I feel like I really need you home more" vs. "*You* have to find a way to be home more." "I" messages are always better received than "you" messages.

4. We can phrase things positively rather than negatively. For example, it's better to say, "I know you're overwhelmed at work, but I really need you home more" as opposed to, "You never want to do anything with me."

5. We can avoid using absolutes such as the word *never* in the previous sentence. Criticism that includes such words as *never* and *always* is likely to induce argument, not invite agreement. It's also generally untrue. There are very few, if any, situations in which our spouse *always* or *never* does something.

6. It helps to be specific in our negative feedback and to make certain that we are talking about specific behavior and not the person. Let's say your spouse has put you down in public and you want to express your feelings about how you were treated. It's better to point to the specific instance as if it were an isolated incident (even if it isn't). "I was hurt tonight when you put me down in front of everybody." Notice that the incident is clearly described, and the feedback is not personal. Such phrasing works a little better than: "You're an insensitive jerk! How could you possibly do that to me? You're always putting me down!"

All of the above suggestions can be helpful and are worth noting as we try to improve ourselves. In fact, much more could be said about each one. But I don't believe the solution to our being less abrasive lies in learning how to phrase things differently. I believe the more complete answer is found in the principles taught in God's marriage manual. George could go to classes, read self-help books, and put good effort into trying to say the right thing. Likely as not, he would still be perceived as being a critical person. He has a good chance of becoming less critical and more effective in his marriage only if he changes entirely the way he views things. If, instead of responding to the things his wife does that irritate him, he were able to think first of her feelings, put himself in her shoes, be more forgiving and humble, kind, loving, and long-suffering—as the scriptures teach—he wouldn't be so inclined to correct her. "Whatsoever ye would that men should do to you, do ye even so to them" (Matthew 7:12) is still the best advice available on this subject.

WHY ARE OTHERWISE GOOD PEOPLE CRITICAL?

George, difficult as he is to live with, is basically a good guy. He tries to do the right thing, and he wants the best for his family. If asked, he would even say he doesn't believe in being critical of others. Then why is he? In part, he is a critical person because his focus is too much on worldly concerns, i.e., whether or not his wife looks better in the red dress. Details of daily life are too important to him. Righteous judgment requires having an eternal perspective, meaning that we focus on the things that really matter, such as eternal values, principles, and relationships. Unrighteous judgments are the products of a temporal and self-centered outlook.

Another, and perhaps more basic reason for George's critical nature, may be found in what might be described as his "carrot and stick" motivational philosophy. In his theory, we achieve if we are threatened with a stick, which usually means criticizing or withholding rewards, which typically comes down to withholding acceptance. George is essentially afraid to be accepting, and offering criticism seems necessary in order to encourage those he loves to achieve their potential. This philosophy has been reinforced over the years by the fact that it works. Cracking the whip and withholding acceptance *can* motivate others, but not without negative side effects, as we've seen in the case of George's marriage.

In line with his philosophy, George is actually quite supportive of his wife when she isn't around. But without knowing exactly why, he finds it difficult to compliment her directly. He also feels compelled by some inner force to point out her faults when he sees them. It's actually painful to him to withhold negative comments when he thinks they are deserved. This all stems from his basic motivational philosophy, one he isn't even fully aware that he has. To do otherwise would be to contradict this basic part of himself.

Becoming less judgmental then, as taught in the

Lord's marriage manual, requires that George adopt a different philosophy. He needs to learn a better way to motivate himself and those he cares about. Fortunately, that better way is also found in God's marriage manual. What George needs to discover is the thing that motivated God Himself to make the ultimate sacrifice, "For God so loved the world, that he gave his only begotten Son, that whosoever believeth in him should not perish, but have everlasting life" (John 3:16). That is the key. Love is the answer. "A new commandment I give unto you, That ye love one another; as I have loved you, that ye also love one another. By this shall all men know that ye are my disciples, if ye have love one to another" (John 13:34-35). And again, "If ye keep my commandments, ye shall abide in my love; even as I have kept my Father's commandments, and abide in his love" (John 15:10).

Love is the most potent motivational force in the universe, and it motivates without producing any negative side effects. We can expect good people to eventually do the right thing because they love God and because they love their fellowman. Beyond that, they love the truth. Assuming we are married to a basically good person—and in my experience that's almost universally true—it's not necessary to browbeat or manipulate our spouse to get him or her to do the right thing. What we need to do is *love* our partner, and through example, teach the truth. Then be patient! If our spouse doesn't come around, he or she doesn't come around; but at least we will have done our part.

Chapter seven explores what it means to love our husband or wife. In the Lord's marriage manual, it's something a bit different from the "Hallmark" definition. But first, in the next chapter, the discussion focuses on keeping our thoughts positive about our spouse and others. Certainly, that is one aspect of what it means to love others.

CHAPTER SIX

KEEP THOUGHTS POSITIVE

The light of the body is the eye; if, there-fore, thine eye be single, thy whole body shall be full of light. But if thine eye be evil, thy whole body shall be full of dark-ness. If, therefore, the light that is in thee be darkness, how great is that darkness!

3 NEPHI 13:22-23

There are probably various ways to inter-pret the teachings of the Savior in the above scripture, but among them is the important concept that what we think controls how we feel and, in turn, how we behave. Those who think evil thoughts become evil in their behavior and per-son. Those who focus on the negative aspects of them-selves and others become negative people. Their whole view is filtered through a negative frame of ref-erence, which darkens their outlook and personality, not to mention causes trouble in their relationships.

Let me share a story that demonstrates how this principle works. One 4th of July I took part of my family waterskiing while my wife stayed home to spend some time with a favorite cousin. As we were bringing the boat in after a day on the water, I stowed the car keys in the pocket of my swimsuit. They seemed secure enough, but when I jumped in the water to help trailer the boat, the car keys fell out of my pocket and went to the bottom of the lake. Several of us madly searched for them in the muck, but to no avail.

I had no extra key, and we were in a remote location, far from any locksmith. Feeling more than a little foolish, I called my wife and asked if she would be willing to bring me a spare set of keys. Essentially, I was asking her to make a three-hour drive (one way), on crowded highways, and to significantly interrupt the day she had planned—all of this because I had been careless with the keys and had provided no backup.

I think a lot of spouses would have been irritated. In fact, I think I might have been irritated if our roles had been reversed. At the very least, my wife would have been justified in asking, "Why weren't you more careful with the keys?" To her credit, she *cheerfully* responded. She chuckled on the phone when I described the problem, but she didn't lecture. She made the long drive, bringing with her a supply of cold drinks and a pleasant attitude. She made the best of things by bringing her cousin along and by focusing on the positive and not the negative aspects of the situation. I don't think she even realized what a positive effect her good attitude had. Her example taught us all how we should act in that kind of situation.

Things might have gotten ugly if my wife had responded negatively, as another woman I know has a habit of doing. Katy is achievement oriented and committed to the gospel. She really is a good person, but she focuses on negatives to the point that her whole life is dreary, and there can be little intimacy in her marriage. She has basically a sour personality, certainly not cheerful.

Consider Joseph Smith's teachings on this subject. Referring to the Saints who had been plundered, murdered, and driven from their homes in Missouri, the Prophet said, "Therefore, dearly beloved brethren, let us *cheerfully* do all things that lie in our power" (D&C 123:17; emphasis added). Even when times are difficult, God's marriage manual suggests the need to maintain a cheerful attitude. Because of her generally negative outlook, this was impossible for Katy.

She even turned things that are basically positive into something negative. For example, Katy loves to ice skate, and she is very good at it. Her husband, on the other hand, is not much of a skater. If given his preference, he would avoid ice skating altogether. But on one occasion he went with Katy to the rink, in an effort to show interest in something that was important to her. At the rink he mostly sat and watched the skaters, making only a few wobbly trips around the ice himself. Against his better judgment, he did attempt to skate with Katy, but that didn't go well because of the great difference in their skating abilities.

On the way home from the outing, Katy was irritated. She was upset that her husband hadn't done more to work on his skill while at the rink. In her opinion, he should have been on the ice the whole time trying to improve his skating technique, just as she had been. She said that to her way of thinking, this was just another example of his general laziness. She also let him know that she had been embarrassed by his clumsiness when they had tried to skate together. Her comment was: "You are a good athlete. If you would just spend a little time and effort you wouldn't look so foolish out there." It irritated her, too, that her own workout hadn't gone well. She had been so worried about what her husband was or wasn't doing that she was unable to concentrate on her own practice. It was hard for her to feel good about her skating unless she improved her ability, at least a little, on each outing. That hadn't happened this time.

Rather than appreciating the effort her husband had made to be supportive, and rather than relishing the opportunity of doing something she loves, Katy had focused on the negative aspects of the outing. That had made the whole experience negative, for both Katy and her husband. Given her attitude, it would probably be a long time before they would go skating together again. In fact, based on the argument that erupted in the car on the way home, it would likely be a while before they would do anything together. In spite of her strong commitment to righteous goals, Katy's eye (viewpoint, focus) was dark and negative, which made her whole personality and her relationship with her husband dark and negative.

It's hard to get close to a prickly pear. It's not easy to be intimate with a judgmental person or to enjoy spending time with a sour personality. In spite of how much she wanted intimacy and a great marriage, Katy's negative outlook made that impossible.

LOOK AT THE DOUGHNUT AND NOT AT THE HOLE.

Katy is an example of someone who consistently looks at the hole and not at the doughnut. There is positive and negative in almost everything in the world, whether we are talking about a skating trip or someone's personality. How we feel about something is controlled by whether we focus on the positive or negative part—the doughnut or the hole. Bob and Sue Hartley are another example of this. Following is a brief list of Bob Hartley's positive and negative attributes:

POSITIVES	NEGATIVES
Good provider	Often critical
Frugal	Wastes too much time watching TV
Law abiding	Sleeps a lot
Goes to church regularly	Rarely does his home teaching
Helps at home when asked	Not a self-starter at home

Two things are of interest here. First, Sue Hartley maintains a very judgmental attitude toward her husband and consistently focuses on his negative characteristics while discounting his strengths. Just as destructive, she lets him and others know on a regular basis what a disappointment he is to her. Second, Bob Hartley is equally hard on himself. He has come to believe that he doesn't have much to offer the world. He, therefore, is more comfortable avoiding interaction with people by sitting in front of the TV, and he neglects such things as his home teaching assignment. Plainly, his negative focus holds him back from good works that he would otherwise do, and it robs him of the motivation to improve his behavior and personality.

One of the classic examples in God's marriage manual of someone concentrating on the doughnut rather than on the hole is found in the eighth chapter of John in the New Testament. A woman was caught in the act of adultery, and her accusers asked Jesus if she should be stoned, as required by the Mosaic law. The Savior's response, you will remember, was, "He that is without sin among you, let him first cast a stone at her" (John 8:7). After the woman's accusers drifted away, convicted by their own consciences, Jesus said to the woman: "Woman, where are those thine accusers? hath no man condemned thee?" When she responded, "No man, Lord," Jesus replied: "Neither do I condemn thee; go, and sin no more" (see John 8:3-11).

In focusing on the good in this woman, the Lord did not ignore the evil. She was required to "go and sin no more." The Lord clearly condemns adultery, even to the point of condemning an adulterous thought (see 3 Nephi 12:27-32), but He didn't condemn this woman. In effect, sin is condemned here, but not the sinner.

Multiple lessons are taught in this scripture. On one hand, the Sue Hartleys of the world are warned not to throw stones. They themselves are certainly not without sin. On the other hand, the Bob Hartleys of the world need to look at their positives and not condemn themselves. If they are involved in sin, it's the sin that is condemned. But there is no need to condemn their basic nature, to overlook their strengths, or to forget the power within each of us to repent. Focusing on the positive is important here for both Bob and Sue because that's the thing that will best facilitate their reaching their ultimate goal of becoming perfect.

Ironically, as suggested in the previous chapter, some people are afraid to focus on the positive, fearing that to do so is to condone the negative. Sue Hartley, for example, was convinced that if she were to be more accepting of her husband, who really was too critical of himself and others, that she would be reinforcing his negative behavior. She actually believed that by criticizing him, she would somehow motivate him to improve. The truth is that her judgmental attitude was holding her husband back.

RIGID, INTOLERANT THINKING

Declaring his intolerance of wrongdoing, the Lord has said, "I the Lord cannot look upon sin with the least degree of allowance" (D&C 1:31). We should be equally firm in condemning sin. However, in doing so, we must take care not to condemn the sinner, nor concentrate on the sin so much that we fail to see the goodness in those who may have broken a commandment. We need to focus on righteousness and goodness so that our whole soul can be filled with light.

As a related concept, I have often wondered exactly what the Lord meant by giving the following instruction: "And again it is written, thou shalt not forswear thyself, but shalt perform unto the Lord thine oaths; But verily, verily, I say unto you, swear not at all; neither by heaven, for it is God's throne; Nor by the earth, for it is his footstool; Neither shalt thou swear by thy head, because thou canst not make one hair black or white, But let your communication be Yea, yea; Nay, nay; for whatsoever cometh of more than these is evil" (3 Nephi 12:33-37). Clearly, the Lord condemns forswearing, i.e., committing perjury or lying under oath, but what about the instruction to "swear not at all"?

"Swearing," as it is used in this context, doesn't refer to the use of profanity. The Lord is warning us instead not to swear oaths, that is, make absolute, binding declarations, such as, "I swear by the memory of my departed mother that . . ." Why? Why such an instruction?

Well, for one thing, as imperfect human beings, our vision is not always clear or our judgments accurate. When, lacking wisdom or not having all the facts, we take any determined course of action, the effects can be disastrous. We all know of situations where someone has made a snap decision based on partial knowledge of a circumstance, has declared their intention to behave in a certain way, and then clung pig-headedly to their point of view—to their own detriment or that of others.

By instructing us not to swear oaths, I believe the Lord is warning us not to make absolute declarations such as we often hear in family relationships, for instance, "You *never* listen to me" or "You *always* have to have your way." Blanket statements such as these are seldom useful in helping to promote harmony or solve problems. And in His marriage manual, the Lord teaches us that since we don't have the wisdom to "swear" to much of anything, it is better not to "swear" at all. This is particularly true when we presume to determine the worth of another human being.

Toni and Bill are newlyweds, just beginning the long-term project of learning how to live together. Shortly after their marriage, they invited Bill's parents over for dinner. Anxious to impress his mom and dad, Bill panicked when he saw Toni peel an orange to add to a fruit salad she was making. Bill's mother never used oranges in fruit salads, and he couldn't believe what his wife was doing. When he called her on it, Toni was offended and insisted on doing it her way. Bill *swore* that it wasn't proper. And the battle was on. His actual words were, "For heaven's sake! [As if heaven cared.] What are you doing? Oranges don't go in a fruit salad!" He wasn't kidding, either. He wanted to make a good impression on his parents, and this was serious business.

As for Toni, she had grown up in a family where oranges were frequently added to a fruit salad. So when Bill swore that she was not properly making the salad, Toni *swore,* "Oh, yes I am!" and they had reached an impasse. They had a heated exchange in which each insisted that his or her point of view was correct, as if the principle involved were of eternal consequence. The problem, of course, was that they both "swore" (i.e., vowed in effect by all that is sacred) that there is only one correct way to make a fruit salad. They would have been so much better off had they "sworn not at all" and each had been able to concede that there might be another way.

THINKING OPTIMISTICALLY

As suggested above, keeping our body full of light involves staying focused on the positive qualities in others and ourselves, and in refraining from making rigid, absolute statements. It also involves thinking optimistically. God's marriage manual encourages cheerfulness, delight, gladness, happiness, pleasure, and joy, even when circumstances combine against us. The means to that end are also defined in the scriptures. Among such suggestions is one from Paul: "For ye had compassion of me in my bonds, and took joyfully the spoiling of your goods, knowing in yourselves that ye have in heaven a better and an enduring substance" (Hebrews 10:34). Paul is here reminding us of an important truth. By focusing on our eternal future, we can be optimistic and joyful even if things are not going well in the present.

Of those who make covenants with Him and honor them, the Lord has said: "And he that receiveth me receiveth my Father; And he that receiveth my Father receiveth my Father's kingdom; therefore all that my Father hath shall be given unto him" (D&C 84:37-38). This profound promise makes the ingredients in a fruit salad look fairly unimportant. When we focus on the longer term, it's a little easier to deal with whatever problems mortal life throws at us.

It's interesting that those who get mired in negative circumstances, and those who have a generally negative, sour, and pessimistic personality, tend to see problems in predictable ways. For one thing, they focus too much on immediate problems and not on the ultimate goal, as discussed above. For another, their darkened spirit causes such persons to view current problems as permanent setbacks. They think, "This will never change." "I'll never be able to fix this." Those who are more optimistic tend to see problems as temporary, feeling, "This too shall pass."

If our outlook is based on the teachings found in God's marriage manual, we will naturally view our marital problems as temporary. Death is as profound a problem as there is in mortality, but the person of faith knows that "in Christ shall all be made alive" (1 Corinthians 15:22). Sin has the potential to create dire and permanent consequences through eternity, but thanks to the Lord's ultimate gift of atonement, even those consequences can be temporary. "Come now, and let us reason together, saith the Lord; though your sins be as scarlet, they shall be as white as snow; though they be red like crimson, they shall be as wool" (Isaiah 1:18).

In addition to viewing problems as being permanent, pessimistic people tend also to see their problems as being pervasive. They say, "This affects everything," as opposed to, "This is a problem, but it doesn't have to affect my whole life." The truth is that even the most trying circumstances don't negate all the positives in our lives. For example, suppose a husband leaves his young wife and their four children for another woman. By any measure, that would be a traumatic, gut-wrenching experience for the young mother—one that has the potential to turn her whole life upside down. But the catastrophic event doesn't immediately negate everything else in her life.

Her faith in God need not be affected. Her relationships with her children, extended family members, and friends can continue. The woman's talents and abilities are not negated. Future opportunities in this life and eternal potential continue. It might seem at the time as though everything is ruined, but that simply isn't true. It is true, however, that the degree of pain she suffers is dictated in part by how she views her situation. Thinking such things as "This too shall pass" and "This is awful, but it doesn't ruin everything" will help limit the pain.

Those following the advice in God's marriage manual are in the best position to avoid becoming pessimistic. Problems are not permanent, nor are they pervasive. With faith in the Lord, there is an ultimate solution to every problem, and having the proper perspective enables us to bear our difficulties without despairing. It takes some effort on our part, however, to remember this in real time as we face challenging situations.

THE MARTHA COMPLEX

The scriptures describe an occasion when Jesus was in the home of Martha and her sister, Mary. Mary sat with the Savior and "heard his word," while Martha busied herself with the formalities and work involved in hosting their important guest. At some point, Martha was "cumbered about much serving" and complained to Jesus that she was serving alone without Mary's help. The Master's response was, "Martha, Martha, thou art careful and troubled about many things: But one thing is needful: and Mary hath chosen that good part, which shall not be taken away from her" (Luke 10:41-42).

Martha needed to place less emphasis on the formalities of her temporal service and more on the spiritual enrichment she might have drawn from Jesus. What she was doing had merit, but it was done at the expense of an opportunity to learn from and relate to the Savior of the World. Obviously we don't have the opportunity to entertain the Lord directly, as Martha did, but the mistake she made is commonly made by good people. Good people sometimes let their commitment to good things, such as outward service and the details of projects, get in the way of more important matters. If they are inordinately concerned about the details involved in daily life, so focused on getting things done, they can easily miss out on the opportunity to learn from others and lose the great benefits available in close relationships. The fact is, building an intimate relationship requires having informal conversations and spending unstructured time together. Some people foolishly consider such things a waste of time.

Examples include the fellow who is so intent on getting his lawn mowed that he is abrupt and short with a neighbor who stops by to talk. Then there is the mother who is so focused on the details of her daughter's wedding that she misses the opportunity to get to know the new in-laws and is short-tempered with her family. Or what about the dad who is so involved with his project that he yells at his young son who interrupts in an attempt to get attention?

Unfortunately, there are otherwise good couples out there whose marriages are sterile and nonintimate because they don't "waste" enough time together. Without continually reminding ourselves of what's really important, as taught in God's marriage manual, it's easy to get off course. When we do, it's hard to keep the positive perspective necessary if we are to be most effective in our family relationships.

CHECKING OUR THINKING

Several suggestions have been given in this chapter on how to keep our souls full of light. The biggest need, of course, is to keep the commandments. If we are involved in evil, at some point we become evil and lose all light. As suggested earlier, however, there are also at least four key things we must do if we are to live a righteous life: (1) We need to keep our thoughts positive by focusing on what's right and not what's wrong. (2) We need to avoid making rigid and absolute statements. (3) We need to remain optimistic by remembering that problems are temporary and are not pervasive. (4) We need to avoid succumbing to the "Martha complex." These concepts from God's marriage manual are all helpful; but following them requires us to be more aware of our thinking than we typically are.

In some cases we aren't conscious of what we are thinking because we are caught up in the emotion of the moment, sometimes because of pride, as Bill and Toni were in an earlier example. Other times, we are detached from our thoughts and unaware of how our minds might be operating on a subconscious level. For instance, we probably have all had the frightening experience of realizing we have driven from point A to point B without giving any conscious thought to the mechanics of doing so.

The fact is, our minds are capable of operating on more than one level at a time. We might, therefore, ask ourselves, "What do I think about when I don't have to think? What am I saying to myself while performing a routine task that doesn't take a lot of concentration? Are my thoughts positive or negative? Do I think in rigid and dogmatic terms? When I encounter a problem, do I treat it as though it were permanent and pervasive?"

Is it possible to control our thoughts and change our patterns of thinking? I believe it is. One function of the Holy Ghost is "to teach the truth" (D&C 50:14), and we can pray to feel the influence of the Spirit—not only with regard to the truths about God and His kingdom, but about ourselves.

A little exercise that some find useful in auditing their thoughts is to put some kind of a reminder in places where it will be randomly encountered through the day. For instance, a signal dot might be attached to a wristwatch or a car's rearview mirror. A note might be tucked into an appointment book, wallet, or purse, or taped in various places around the house or office. Such reminders can serve as cues that remind us to tune into what we are thinking.

If we become aware that our thoughts are negative and destructive, then we can attempt to control or get rid of them. That sounds easy to do, but we know from sad experience that it is not. Here, again, we have not been left alone. Humble petitioners will receive God's help as they persist in their efforts to change the way they think. In this way, God's marriage manual is like no other in the world. It is a set of instructions that comes with a number to call for immediate help.

CHAPTER SEVEN

LOVE, COVENANTS, AND PATIENCE

———

A new commandment I give unto you,
That ye love one another; as I have loved
you, that ye also love one another. By
this shall all men know that ye are my
disciples, if ye have love one to another.

JOHN 13:34–35

Nowhere is the Lord's commandment to love one another more important, or more severely tested, than in family relationships. The requirement that marriage partners love each other is made clear by the Lord. "Thou shalt love thy wife with all thy heart, and shalt cleave unto her and none else" (D&C 42:22). But what is love as taught in God's marriage manual? In popular culture, love in marriage is usually defined as a strong, passionate affection for one another, based in large part on sexual attraction.

That's how Barry defined it, but sadly he knew

that he was *not* in love with Laurie that way. Barry married Laurie a little later in life than normal, after going through a very careful decision process. He knew he wasn't particularly attracted to Laurie physically, but she had so many positive qualities that he decided to marry on those grounds, hoping that physical attraction either wouldn't matter or would come later. Unfortunately, it didn't come later, and it did matter.

It mattered because Barry thought that it did. By defining love in a passionate, romantic sense, he was not able to honestly say that he loved Laurie. That created anxiety and discomfort each of the many times the issue came up. Wedding anniversaries, birthdays, Valentine's Days, and other special occasions when expressions of love were expected were difficult. It was also uncomfortable for Barry whenever Laurie expressed her love to him. He felt obligated to return the sentiment, but he couldn't do so in good conscience. Handholding and hugs were awkward, and his sexual relationship with Laurie was strained. The absence of physical attraction was most noticeable in their intimate life.

No matter how hard he tried, Barry was not able to develop a feeling of passionate, romantic love that he felt he should have for his wife. He was attracted to other women in that way, but not to Laurie. Barry took his problem to his bishop, who gave him some excellent advice based on God's marriage manual. In God's book, love is a verb. It connotes action, not feeling. We love others in that we serve them. We treat them kindly and are not judgmental. We have their best interests at heart. Love is essentially the sum of all God's commandments. We love others when we try to treat them in a way compatible with all His directives.

President Spencer W. Kimball further underscores this definition: "Love is unselfish. For many years I saw a strong man carry his tiny, emaciated, arthritic wife to meetings and wherever she could go. There could be no sexual expression. Here was selfless indication of affection. I think that is pure love. I saw a kindly woman wait on her husband for many years as he deteriorated with muscular dystrophy. She waited on him hand and foot, night and day, when all he could do was to blink his eyes in thanks. I believe that was love." (*The Teachings of Spencer W. Kimball,* ed. Edward W. Kimball [1982], 245).

The people described by President Kimball above were most likely not physically attracted to their partner under the circumstances, but they were still demonstrating the essence of love. In this way, Barry also loved Laurie. After working at it and using the Lord's definition, he was finally able to honestly say to his wife that he loved her, even though the feelings that he had previously attached to those words were not there. Fortunately, this change of definition greatly improved Barry's comfort level with his wife. No more did he feel hypocritical, and he was no longer tongue-tied when it came time to say "I love you." As he came to understand what love really is, as defined in scripture, Barry also gained an important perspective about his being attracted to other women.

As a single man, prior to his marriage to Laurie, Barry had found himself attracted to many women. He would settle on a steady girlfriend, but soon his interest would cool and someone else would start looking very good to him. Barry assumed that this tendency would end with marriage to the "right woman." Since it didn't end after his marriage to Laurie, he assumed, incorrectly, that she was not the right one. That conclusion by itself was very destructive to the marriage, but it went beyond that. By his definition, Barry's romantic and often passionate interest in other women *was* love. It was something he felt he needed in his life, and its absence in his marriage meant that something essential was missing.

With his new understanding, Barry realized that much of what he had thought of as love was actually lust. Barry had always defined lust as an unrighteous interest in something evil, which it is. But he failed to see the connection between that definition and what was happening in his life. He didn't spend a great deal of time fantasizing about having sex with other women, which he would immediately have recognized as lust. But Barry had let physical attraction become much too important to him.

Barry was also coveting the intensity and excitement typical of new relationships. (See chapter four.) He was coveting the thrill of something new, especially something forbidden. He had succumbed to a "grass is greener" perspective. The interest he took in other women was not something desirable from a righteous perspective, and his lusting actually contradicted his marriage vows and put him at moral risk. In essence, it was much more like lust than love.

Barry experienced somewhat of a jolt as he saw himself in the warning given in 1 John 2:15: "Love not the world, neither the things that are in the world. If any man love the world, the love of the Father is not in him. For all that is in the world, the lust of the flesh, and the lust of the eyes, and the pride of life, is not of the Father, but is of the world."

By labeling things correctly, Barry was better able to eliminate the attention he was tempted to pay to other women. He was also able to abandon his unsuccessful and frustrating attempt to make Laurie into a sensual object. All he had to do was focus on loving her in the Lord's way. By making these attitude changes, physical attraction was no longer so critical for Barry, and he knew that it would ultimately become a nonissue altogether.

Brigham Young said: "Those who attain to the blessing of the first or celestial resurrection will be pure and holy, and perfect in body. Every man and woman that reaches to this unspeakable attainment will be as beautiful as the angels that surround the throne of God. If you can by faithfulness in this life obtain the right to come up in the morning of the resurrection, you need entertain no fears that the wife will be dissatisfied with her husband, or the husband with the wife, for those of the first resurrection will be free from sin and from the consequences and power of sin" (*Contributor* 9:240).

Barry's new outlook, based on a better understanding of the principle in God's marriage manual, helped him draw closer to Laurie. And it gave him the motivation to commit to his marriage and begin to seriously work on the problems that still existed there. The final chapter in their story has yet to be written, but so far their relationship has improved dramatically. Barry's original decision to marry Laurie has been vindicated.

As a last thought on the subject, to his credit, Barry was a naturally loving person. He simply needed to recognize what love is as defined in God's marriage manual. Others do not naturally love. Some of us are selfish and must stretch ourselves to meet the Lord's requirement. Spencer W. Kimball has given hope to those in this category. He said: "One can learn to be loving. If one patterns his life in the mold of love—if he consciously and determinedly directs his thoughts, controls his acts, and tries to feel and constantly express his love, he becomes a person of love, for 'As he thinketh in his heart, so is he'" (Proverbs 23:7). (*The Teachings of Spencer W. Kimball,* ed. Edward W. Kimball [1982], 245-46).

THE MARRIAGE COVENANT

The adjustment in Barry's thinking, outlined above, came just in time. He was perilously close to violating the marriage covenant he had made. In God's marriage manual, marriage is described as a covenant between a man and a woman, and also between a couple and God (see D&C 132:19). The husband and wife promise to be true and faithful to each other, and they both promise to be true and faithful to God. God's promise, in return, is that the marriage bond will be eternal and the couple will have the profound opportunity of a "continuation of the seeds forever and ever."

Understanding that marriage is a solemn covenant is an important defense against divorce. Elder Joseph Fielding Smith said: "No marriage should be entered into only in the spirit of prayer and with the holy desire to serve the Lord. When the proper perspective is had divorce cannot come. It was never intended that divorce should be, and the Lord said it was only because of the hardness of the hearts of the people that it did occur. When a young couple is married for time and for all eternity, and each loves the other [keep in mind the definition of love given above], there is an incentive to serve the Lord, and there comes an abiding love for offspring which should carry them through all the difficulties and differences peculiar to mortal life. The husband should religiously respect the rights and wishes of the wife, and the wife, likewise, the husband. Marriage should be considered a sacred covenant, not a convenience or something merely to satisfy lust under legal protection" (*Church History and Modern Revelation,* 2 vols. [1953], 2:358; emphasis added).

Of course, the actions of one spouse sometimes force divorce on the other. The fact of divorce is absolute evidence that at least one partner has broken the marriage covenant. It is not necessarily evidence that they both have. Just the same, anyone contemplating divorce should take a prayerful look at

Matthew 19:3–9. That and other scriptures make clear the sacred and inviolable nature of the marriage covenant.

BREAKING THE COVENANT

In spite of the covenant nature of marriage, too many decide to end their relationship for insufficient cause. Some decide that they just aren't happy with their mate. Others say they have fallen out of love with their partner, or perhaps they claim never to have loved him or her in the first place (as did Barry in the previous example). Still others decide that they have fallen in love with someone else and can't be happy unless they leave their marriage for the other person.

What's more, some who divorce for such reasons are active Church members who claim that they have prayed about it and have received a personal revelation confirming their choice. What's going on here? Does God condone divorce? Given what the scriptures say about the evils of divorce, over the years I've come to believe that these personal "revelations" are often the products of wishful thinking and not inspiration from God. No doubt the individual has an emotional experience not unlike personal revelation, but it's *not* necessarily a message from God.

On the one hand, the assumed revelation might originate with Satan. Elder Joseph Fielding Smith has pointed out that: "We should be on guard always to resist Satan's advances. He will appear to us in the person of a friend or a relative in whom we have confidence. He has power to place thoughts in our minds and to whisper to us in unspoken impressions to entice us to satisfy our appetites or desires and in various other ways he plays upon our weaknesses and desires" (*Answers to Gospel Questions*, comp. Joseph Fielding Smith Jr., 5 vols. [1957–66], 3:81).

On the other hand, perhaps we are simply confusing ourselves because of our emotional involvement in the situation. Personal revelation is so closely related to ordinary emotional experience that it's easy to get confused. This is especially true if we are not living worthily at the time, which is usually the case with those who receive questionable revelations.

Fortunately, the Lord has provided help for us when we are trying to interpret what seem to be spiritual impressions. First of all, there is the written word. The standard works are called such because they provide a standard against which to measure our beliefs and behavior. True, personal revelation has contradicted scripture a time or two (see Nephi's being inspired to kill Laban, for example: 1 Nephi 4:10–13), but those instances are exceptionally rare. Typically, we can know we are being misled if our impressions contradict the doctrine taught in the standard works.

Furthermore, we can be confident that our impressions are misleading if they contradict the testimony of priesthood leaders. These testimonies may come to us in written form through conference talks or other addresses. Or they may come in the form of counsel from an immediate priesthood leader. Either way, if we are humble enough, we can know when we are being misled by spurious revelation.

The record itself is clear. The Lord Himself, His ancient prophets, and His current prophets have all emphasized that marriage is a sacred obligation that cannot be ended except under very special circumstances. Among modern-day prophets, President David O. McKay has said: "Except in cases of infidelity or other extreme conditions, the Church frowns upon divorce, and authorities look with apprehension upon the increasing number of divorces among members of the Church. . . . In the light of scripture, ancient and modern, we are justified in concluding that Christ's ideal pertaining to marriage is the unbroken home, and conditions that cause divorce are violations of his divine teachings" (*Gospel Ideals* [1954], 469–70).

President Joseph Fielding Smith said: "If all mankind would live in strict obedience to the gospel, and in that love which is begotten by the Spirit of the

Lord, all marriages would be eternal, divorce would be unknown. Divorce is not part of the gospel plan and has been introduced because of the hardness of heart and unbelief of the people. . . . Those who violate this sacred and solemn covenant are going to have a sorry time of it if they are guilty when they come to the judgement seat of God, for they have broken the bands of an eternal union and lost their promise of exaltation in the kingdom of God" (*Doctrines of Salvation,* comp. Bruce R. McConkie, 3 vols. [1954–56], 2:80).

This is straight talk. Divorce is sometimes the only recourse, but it is never a good thing. A person is justified in divorcing only when his or her partner has broken the marriage covenant through adultery or is guilty of some other heinous or destructive behavior. Falling out of love with one's partner or falling in love with someone else or just being tired of living with one's mate does not justify divorce. This is true no matter how a person feels after praying and fasting about the issue.

WHY A COVENANT?

God's marriage manual makes marriage a solemn commitment in part because of the harmful ramifications of divorce. Most people who have not gone through a divorce underestimate its expense. The spiritual, emotional, and financial costs are in fact astronomical. This is particularly true when children are involved. In that case, all of society loses. The dramatic increase in the number of single-parent families in recent years is matched by an equally dramatic rise in crime, violence, drug use, and youth pathologies and misbehaviors. God knows that the best model for child rearing is the two-parent family, preferably one in which Mom and Dad are the natural or adopted parents and where Mom stays home with the children.

Another reason for the Lord's long-range perspective on marriage is that it takes a long time for a great relationship to develop. Actually, relationships are often satisfying, even exciting, early on, when both partners are still enthralled with each other and when they are on their best behavior. Soon, however, couples tend to become disenchanted with each other and lose focus on their relationship. At that point, the real work and great opportunity in marriage begin. Determined commitment is what holds a couple through the middle stage (which might last most of a lifetime) until they have both grown to their potential. None of us are done yet. We are all becoming. It's a shame when a couple isn't able to see the process through. Those who divorce to pursue another relationship usually don't find the nirvana they expect, but rather must begin the difficult process of growing together all over again with someone new. Moreover, they carry with them to the new relationship the emotional baggage that may have contributed to the divorce. There is no guarantee the second time will be any easier than the first.

I suppose a third reason that the Lord considers marriage to be a sacred commitment is the holy nature of the institution. Marriage follows an eternal model and has eternal potential. Most readers are probably familiar with section 132 of the Doctrine and Covenants, which makes all of this clear.

Think of the least flashy couple you know who have been married in the temple. These might be quiet people who do their Church callings without fanfare and who lack worldly credentials or accomplishments. This same couple, assuming they keep their marriage covenant, and their covenant to keep the commandments of God generally, have this promise: "Then shall they be gods, because they have no end; therefore shall they be from everlasting to everlasting, because they continue; then shall they be above all, because all things are subject unto them. Then shall they be gods, because they have all power, and the angels are subject unto them" (D&C 132:20).

That's an overwhelming promise open to all couples who are willing to make this commitment.

Naturally, however, couples must prove absolutely worthy of such power and status before such honors will ever be granted. We demonstrate our worthiness by how we honor our covenants.

IT'S WORTH IT.

We all need to keep the covenant nature of marriage in mind as we contemplate or participate in it. I have known people, however, who were so convinced of the sacred nature of marriage and the importance of keeping their covenant that they refused to make the covenant in the first place. Sam was thirty-seven years old and had never married. He was healthy, well employed, and marriageable in every way. He had also had many opportunities to marry. But each time he got close to someone, he would back off or sabotage the relationship. When analyzed, it became obvious that Sam's main problem was fear of committing. In his view, the decision was so important and so final that he felt he had to be absolutely sure of his choice. Since a person controls only half the outcome in a marriage, no one can absolutely know going in that his or her marriage will work. When last encountered, Sam was still waiting to know for sure.

Sam's level of anxiety wasn't lessened by the following declaration in God's marriage manual: "But whoso breaketh this covenant after he hath received it, and altogether turneth therefrom, shall not have forgiveness of sins in this world nor in the world to come" (D&C 84:41). This warning has to do specifically with the oath and covenant of the priesthood, but it's reasonable to assume that those who break their marriage covenant are in similar trouble. (See D&C 132:4–5, for example.) Certainly, breaking one's marriage covenant is something that can't be done with impunity.

But then, in the next verse in the Doctrine and Covenants, is found the following: "And wo unto all those who come not unto this priesthood which ye have received" (84:42). This corresponds with another statement made by the Lord regarding eternal marriage: "Verily, verily, I say unto you, except ye abide my law ye cannot attain to this glory" (D&C 132:21). Those who make priesthood covenants and break them will have problems. But then so will those who refuse to make covenants in the first place. They will also lose their opportunity for exaltation.

When it comes time to marry, at some point, after giving the matter prayerful consideration, it makes sense to close our eyes and jump. As we do our best to honor our covenants, we then trust in the Lord to help us make it work.

THE NEED FOR PATIENCE

Actually, once married we need to do our best to honor our covenants, trust in the Lord to give us the help we need, *and be patient.* What Paul said about life certainly applies to marriage: "Let us run with patience the race that is set before us" (Hebrews 12:1). Regarding patience, President Joseph F. Smith observed: "We want things a long time before we get them, and the fact that we wanted them a long time makes them all the more precious when they come. In nature we have our seedtime and harvest; and if children were taught that the desires that they sow may be reaped by and by through patience and labor, they will learn to appreciate whenever a long-looked-for goal has been reached. Nature resists us and keeps admonishing us to wait; indeed, we are compelled to wait" (*Gospel Doctrine,* 5th ed. [1939], 298).

A great marriage doesn't just happen because two people made a fortuitous choice in a marriage partner. It occurs over time as the result of lessons learned from mistakes, services rendered to each other, and experiences shared. In that way, it's a lot like seedtime and harvest—except there is usually a longer interval between the planting and the reaping. Looking at a beautiful field of wheat in the fall, even a nonfarmer recognizes that the wheat didn't just happen to grow as it did. The crop is the result of many hours of careful attention, and perhaps even more than a little sweat and a few tears. A great marriage is achieved in the same way.

Patience is required on at least two levels. First is the requirement to be patient with our partner's imperfections. Most criticism, nagging, and demanding behavior, which are all so destructive in relationships (see chapter five), result from impatience. Needed improvements just aren't happening fast enough. At another level, we need to be patient with the slow development of the relationship itself. It's easy to forget that it takes time. We often compare our relationship to some ideal and become discouraged at the contrast. We look at the beautiful field of wheat and think that it's too much work, or it will take too long, or it's not even possible in our case.

It is possible, but it does take time and effort. President Ezra Taft Benson emphasized the need for us to keep trying and to be patient: "A priesthood holder is to be patient. Patience is another form of self-control. It is the ability to postpone gratification and to bridle one's passions. In his relationships with loved ones, a patient man does not engage in impetuous behavior that he will later regret. Patience is composure under stress. A patient man is understanding of other's faults. A patient man also waits on the Lord.

We sometimes read or hear of people who seek a blessing from the Lord, then grow impatient when it does not come swiftly. Part of the divine nature is to trust in the Lord enough to 'be still, and know that [He is] God' (D&C 101:16). A priesthood holder who is patient will be tolerant of the mistakes and failings of his loved ones. Because he loves them, he will not find fault nor criticize nor blame" ("Godly Characteristics of the Master," *Ensign,* November 1986, 47).

WHAT GETS IN THE WAY OF PATIENCE?

It's easy to see that patience is an important virtue, yet lots of otherwise virtuous people aren't very patient, especially with their loved ones. In fact, it's striking how patient some are outside their family, but how impatient they are with those they love. Marietta is an example. She works with young women in her ward and is well loved and respected by all the Laurels she advises—except her daughter. The mother-daughter relationship is strained, in large part, because Marietta is so impatient at home.

To illustrate the contrast, when one of the Laurels in her group became pregnant out of wedlock, Marietta was extremely compassionate and understanding. She spent long hours tenderly counseling this young lady and encouraging her to put her life in order. She cried with her, hugged her, and otherwise showed support. On the other hand, when her daughter came home with her first "C" in a high school class, Marietta was all over her. Her response to her daughter was harsh, insensitive, and discouraging. She was more angry than concerned and more demeaning than supportive.

Likewise, if one of the Laurels dropped the ball on an assignment, Marietta would try to teach responsibility, but she would do so in a kind and sensitive manner. By contrast, if her daughter was late getting to a chore, Marietta often yelled at her and complained about her laziness. She was quick to complain about the quality of her daughter's efforts whenever they fell short of her standard and was slow to recognize good effort when it occurred.

So why the contrast? Most likely Marietta is impatient at home because she takes her daughter's mistakes personally. With other people, she feels obligated to teach and help them when they have a problem, but she does not feel responsible for the problem or its solution. With her daughter, she feels responsible for both the problem and the solution. When her daughter's grades dropped, in Marietta's mind, it was as though she had failed as a mother, and she felt compelled to somehow see to it that her daughter's grades improved. When her daughter acted irresponsibly, it felt to Marietta as though she had failed to teach her daughter properly. Marietta also then felt obligated to make sure that her daughter became more responsible.

By taking responsibility for her daughter's problems and their solutions, Marietta was assuming responsibility for something she couldn't control. In this way she had set herself up for frustration, which led to anger and impatience. By taking her daughter's mistakes personally, Marietta tended to overreact to them, which also contributed to her impatience. All this made for a strained relationship with her daughter, which led to less cooperation than she might have otherwise experienced. This too added to Marietta's frustration and impatience.

The solution for Marietta was to better understand her parental role as taught in God's marriage manual. Marietta is surely responsible to teach her daughter, and she will be held accountable if she does not (see D&C 68:25). She is not responsible, however, for whether or not her daughter follows those teachings. This understanding derives from one of the fundamental principles taught in the scriptures; namely, the principle of agency. This principle is so important that Lucifer and a good number of others were expelled from the presence of God because they chose not to support it (see Moses 4:3). Agency allows

Marietta's daughter to make choices independent of her mother, and for which her mother is not responsible. Because of this principle, Mom needs to teach, but she cannot rightly force compliance with her teachings.

Just as many other good people, Marietta honors this principle more easily with those outside her home, than she does with the members of her own family. If she were to follow it at home, it would be much easier for her to be as patient with her daughter as she is in her dealings with her Laurels. The great benefits of living patiently could then be realized. This is also true of Marietta's relationship with her husband. Her impatience with him is also a significant problem in the family.

With her husband, however, Marietta's impatience is due more to good, old-fashioned vanity and selfishness. For example, she is impatient with her husband's weight and failure to do any physical exercise. She has told herself that she is only concerned about his physical health. But the truth is that his appearance embarrasses her. She is also worried about him having a heart attack, not so much because of its effect on him, but because of how it would affect her. Much of the time her impatience with her husband boils down to concern about what others will think or how she will be impacted by his problem.

Again, the solution lies in better following the advice in God's marriage manual. Vanity and selfishness are clearly to be avoided. Marietta would also benefit from better applying the advice given in the Beatitudes. These are the declarations of blessedness offered by the Savior in the Sermon on the Mount, as discussed in the next chapter.

CHAPTER EIGHT

THE BEATITUDES AND FAMILIES

———

These declarations of the Master are known in the literature of the Christian world as the Beatitudes and have been referred to by Bible commentators as the preparation necessary for entrance into the kingdom of heaven. For the purposes of this discussion may I speak of them as something more than that as they are applied to you and me. They embody, in fact, the constitution for a perfect life.

HAROLD B. LEE,
STAND YE IN HOLY PLACES (1974), 343

The eight declarations of blessedness found in the Sermon on the Mount in some ways duplicate principles discussed in prior chapters. Because of their importance, however, it seems worthwhile to state each of the beatitudes here, along with a brief summary of how the

principle affects family relationships. The Beatitudes
can be found in Matthew 5 and in the Joseph Smith
Translation of Matthew 5. They are also found in the
Book of Mormon in 3 Nephi 12. The Book of Mormon
account is the one used for this discussion.

> *Yea, blessed are the poor in spirit who come
> unto me, for theirs is the kingdom of heaven
> (3 Nephi 12:3).*

To be poor in spirit means to recognize one's
dependence on the Lord. A person poor in spirit
instinctively prays for help with life issues. Such a person gratefully accepts the direction offered in the
scriptures and the guidance received through personal revelation. The result is that those who are poor
in spirit are much more likely than anyone else to
ensure that their behavior conforms to the counsel
given in God's marriage manual.

Although from a distance it certainly doesn't
appear so, Ray is a person lacking this kind of humility. He is a good person who generally tries to live the
teachings of the Lord, at least as he understands
them. Ray is well read in the scriptures and prays
daily. He can repeat the Beatitudes and many other
scriptures from memory. In most ways his behavior
conforms to the gospel, but there is a problem. Ray is
addicted to pornography. His wife occasionally

discovers his hidden magazines or videos, and she has also walked in on Ray while he was accessing pornographic images from the Internet.

Ray's wife is justifiably offended by his vice. Having her husband lust after other women (albeit in fantasy) is a form of infidelity. It cheapens their relationship, and it is a breech of trust and commitment, similar in spirit and intent to an actual affair. It also leaves his wife feeling physically inadequate. Unlike those of the models Ray salivates over, his wife's body shows the signs of age and of having given birth to five children. In spite of Ray's rationalizations, the overall effect of his habit on his marriage is negative and considerable.

Ray's rationalizations follow a familiar pattern. He has convinced himself that his is a minor sin since it's something he does in private. He recognizes the damage done when his wife discovers or rediscovers his secret, but he thinks of that as *her* problem. If she were more forgiving and less judgmental, there would be no problem in his marriage. Ray has also decided that what he is doing is infinitely preferable to having an actual affair. There is no chance of contracting a communicable disease, and there is no actual adultery. In his view, the thought is certainly a long way from the deed, and his behavior is, therefore, harmless and inconsequential.

From time to time, Ray's ability to rationalize his behavior has diminished, and filled with guilt, he has tried to overcome his problem. But then within a short time he has fallen back, and is left again with the burden of trying to convince himself that his behavior is not that big a deal. Over time, his rationalizations have been buttressed by the fact that, except for his marriage, things are going reasonably well in his life. He even feels as though he is able to draw upon the Spirit when he teaches his Sunday School class and at other times. He is convinced this could not happen if he were guilty of serious sin.

Ray also holds a temple recommend. He has convinced himself that he is morally clean at some basic level, even if perhaps he is technically not so. Whatever his moral status, he has decided that his temple work is of value in any event. Beyond that, he doesn't want to hurt his wife by admitting his problem during worthiness interviews. In spite of his problem (addiction), he sees himself as a loving person who is otherwise faithful and committed to the gospel. He even flatters himself that he is considerate of his wife's feelings, though he is clearly not.

Ray has a problem of course. His rationalizations amount to "rational lies." His habit may in fact be less serious than an actual affair, but indulging himself is still lustful and his behavior constitutes a significant sin. Though he may also occasionally receive spiritual guidance, there is no question but what his habit interferes with his spirituality. There is also no doubt but what it detracts from his marriage. His wife is adversely affected, and Ray himself is also negatively influenced. He is more critical of his wife than he would otherwise be and is conditioned by his behavior to be somewhat dissatisfied with the relationship.

The "poor in spirit who come unto me" seek and then accept the Lord's direction in their lives. Ray seeks the Lord's guidance but then rejects it when that guidance conflicts with his desires. He would have a hard time admitting it, but he is clearly acting as if he knows better than the Lord does. As a result, Ray's marriage is shaky, and he is less effective in his family than he could be. Just as with most "victimless sins," others beside Ray suffer because of his addiction. Heading the list of other victims are his wife and children.

> *And again, blessed are all they that mourn,*
> *for they shall be comforted (3 Nephi 12:4).*

There are at least two ways in which the ability to mourn blesses families. The first has to do with our ability to mourn for our sins. The key here is to have "godly sorrow [that] worketh repentance" (see 2 Corinthians

7:10). In the case of Ray, the simplest solution to the difficulties his addiction causes in his family would be for Ray to repent. If he sincerely mourned because of his sins, repentance would be likely. Unfortunately, Ray was more upset that his sin had been uncovered than he was about the sin itself. Not feeling "godly sorrow," he also lacked the motivation to repent. In general, sin is the most destructive force in our family relationships. Mourning our sins is one of the best guarantees that we will do the necessary work of repentance.

The prophet Alma describes another way in which mourning is important in family relationships. Alma points out that we should be willing to "bear one another's burdens, that they may be light; Yea, and [be] willing to mourn with those that mourn; yea, and comfort those that stand in need of comfort" (Mosiah 18:9). This is an important facet of intimate relationships that sometimes gets overlooked.

Adele expected and hoped that she could share her disappointments with her husband. That was the case when her father died and she mourned his death. Her husband seemed to instinctively know what to say and do, and Adele was grateful to have his listening ear and moral support. At other times though, it just didn't seem to work. When Adele had a bad day with the kids, her husband didn't seem to want to hear it. He would usually criticize Adele for letting them get to her or he would offer advice on how she should handle them differently. Either way, Adele felt alone and misunderstood. She learned not to share her feelings on those days.

Likewise when Adele was hurting because of an offense given her at church or in the neighborhood, her husband would typically show little empathy. Rather, he often seemed disinterested. Or if interested, he was full of advice regarding how she should respond to the situation. When he gave advice, it frequently felt to Adele as though he was almost taking the side of the one who had offended her. Comments such as "You shouldn't let this get you down" or "I don't think it's such a big deal" or "You're overreacting" always led to this feeling.

At one point, Adele was diagnosed as having muscular dystrophy. Her symptoms appeared on a random basis. Some days she was fine, but on others she was barely able to function. This diagnosis and her symptoms were obviously traumatic for Adele, but her husband wasn't very helpful. He acted as though he was angry with her for being sick. He refused to talk about the problem; and he sometimes said things that led her to believe that he thought she was simply malingering.

Adele's husband was able to express sorrow, grieve with her, and show support in certain unusual situations, such as the death of her father. Unfortunately, he was not able to be supportive in other more mundane situations that came up regularly. And why not? The simplest explanation is that he felt obligated to offer suggestions when his wife had a problem. He thought that's what a supportive spouse does. In thinking this way, he was missing an important message in God's marriage manual. It's important to mourn with those that mourn, not to somehow get them over their mourning. Those who are hurting are often helped if we acknowledge their hurt, but rarely are they helped by our advice, especially if our advice is not solicited.

When Adele's husband seemed to be put out by her problems on occasion it was because they often came at a time when he was tired. At those times, Adele's hurting seemed to be just another problem he now had to solve. When he seemed to lack interest in Adele's complaints, it was usually because he wasn't sure how to help her. He was therefore quiet and uncommunicative. Both problems would have disappeared if he had realized that all he basically needed to do was acknowledge her pain. This could be easily accomplished by providing a noncritical, listening ear and a sympathetic shoulder on which to cry. That is, he needed to mourn with those who mourn.

> *And blessed are the meek, for they shall inherit the earth (3 Nephi 12:5).*

The meek are those who are not easily provoked or irritated. They tend to be forgiving when offended. Along with those given in previous chapters, one more example seems appropriate here of how this works in a marriage relationship. Karen and Jim live a long way from their extended families, and their families live far apart. They would like to visit both families for the holidays, but that isn't possible. Both Jim and Karen feel that there are compelling reasons that his or her family should be visited on the upcoming holiday. Karen's mother has not been feeling well, and Karen would like to visit her parents for that reason. Jim's folks are elderly and may not be around for many more holidays. He feels that their situation ought to take priority.

Without a demonstration of meekness, this situation could get ugly. Jim might attack Karen for her selfishness and insensitivity to his needs. Or Karen might criticize Jim on similar grounds. They might try to manipulate each other with threats or ill treatment. They might each take an unbending, stubborn stand that would, in the end, guarantee that neither got what he or she wanted.

By practicing meekness, they would begin from the position that each has a point. They wouldn't waste energy trying to deny the other's claim. If one or the other seemed a little selfish, they would look past the character flaw and focus on the good in the partner. They would be open to compromise and willing to discuss the issue in a fair-minded way until they found a solution that would work for both parties. Neither would dogmatically stick to one choice and one choice only.

At the same time, both Jim and Karen would be open about their wishes and they would not accept a solution totally unacceptable to them. Being meek does not mean being a doormat or a yes-person. Jesus Christ is the best example of meekness, as well as of all other positive character traits. He demonstrated that wonderful mix of forgiveness, tolerance, and long-suffering, but not at the expense of strength of character and integrity with regard to values. Jim and Karen can go and do likewise.

And blessed are all they who do hunger and thirst after righteousness, for they shall be filled with the Holy Ghost (3 Nephi 12:6).

Common dilemmas like the one faced by Karen and Jim often require creativity in order to resolve them in a way that works for everyone. Nothing stifles creativity quicker than closed-minded stubbornness. On the other hand, the wisdom available through the Holy Ghost can greatly assist a couple seeking to derive creative solutions to their problems. That gift, we are promised, comes to those who hunger and thirst after righteousness.

We have all been hungry or thirsty at one time or another and so we can relate to the Lord's metaphor. At those times, not much was more important than eating or drinking. Likewise, righteousness needs to be a primary motive and something always at the forefront of our thinking. In other words, the most important thing to us should always be to do what's right, even if it isn't comfortable at the moment. If that's our primary focus, we can't go far wrong; and we will have the help we need in knowing what the right thing is.

In family relationships, a few things are always right. For example, it's always right to forgive, even if it's not comfortable at the moment. And physical or sexual abuse is never acceptable, no matter what. But otherwise, there are many shades of gray. Should I discipline my child, or let him off with a warning? Should I complain to my spouse about some issue, or just let it go? Do I need to serve my partner, or is this one of those times when I need to take care of myself?

With respect to this last question, there are times when it is appropriate to be a little selfish. This goes along with not running "faster than [we have] strength" (Mosiah 4:27), as discussed earlier. In order to have plenty for others, it is sometimes necessary to stop and refill our own bucket. The problem is that focusing on doing so can easily get out of hand. The key is balance, which takes constant awareness and adjustment.

Family relationships provide an ongoing series of questions such as those suggested. Wouldn't it be wonderful if we had a direct connection to a database that included the truth of all things? Maybe we could access the database through an Internet site, or perhaps we could use an 800-telephone number. As great as this would be, the promise of the Lord actually goes one better. Those who hunger and thirst after righteousness will be filled with the Holy Ghost, "And by the power of the Holy Ghost ye may know the truth of all things" (Moroni 10:5). It's not even necessary to boot up the computer or pick up the phone. It is necessary, however, to be dedicated to and focused on doing the right thing in our lives.

> **And blessed are the merciful, for they shall obtain mercy (3 Nephi 12:7).**

In the overall scheme of things, mercy and justice go together. The prophet Alma probably said it as well as anyone: "What, do ye suppose that mercy can rob justice? I say unto you, Nay; not one whit. If so, God would cease to be God" (Alma 42:25). In God's dealings with us we receive mercy to the extent that we repent, otherwise justice must be served. In our dealings with others, however, mercy is to be emphasized, even if at the expense of justice. This is particularly true in a marriage relationship.

In an earlier example, Ray had a problem with pornography. Ray thought that since the Lord knows the intent of his heart, and since Ray was generally trying to do the right thing, the Lord would therefore certainly understand and forgive him. Unfortunately for Ray, that notion is not supported in God's marriage manual. President Spencer W. Kimball said: "The Lord may temper justice with mercy, but he will never supplant it. Mercy can never replace justice. God is merciful, but he is also just" (*The Miracle of Forgiveness* [1969], 359).

For her part, Ray's wife needed to emphasize mercy. When she first became aware of the problem, Ray's wife, Abigail, reacted by becoming irate and indignant. Ray wasn't taking the problem seriously, so Abigail went to the bishop for him. Essentially she demanded that the bishop do something about Ray's sin. Further, Abigail lectured Ray on the evils of pornography and gave him extensive material to read on the detrimental effects of the habit. Abigail also refused to sleep with Ray and moved to a separate bedroom. She said that she couldn't be comfortable with him sexually under the circumstance, which was partially true; but her primary motive was clearly to make him pay for his sin. Abigail wanted justice done.

The result was predictable. Abigail was miserable. The hurt she experienced as a victim of this form of infidelity was greatly compounded by her anger. She was frustrated that Ray didn't seem to be repentant and that the bishop didn't react as strongly as she thought he should have. Her attempts to punish her husband threatened her marriage and created more of a gulf between them. Naturally, Abigail blamed all of this on her husband, but the reality was that her own actions were a significant factor in both her personal grief and in the problem in their marriage.

Abigail would have been much better off if she had followed the Lord's direction. She needed to show mercy to her husband and leave justice to the Lord.

> *And blessed are all the pure in heart, for they*
> *shall see God (3 Nephi 12:8).*

The word *heart* as used in the scriptures most often seems to refer to the center of a person, i.e., one's core values, beliefs, and motives. By that definition, Abigail in the prior example was not pure in heart with respect to her husband. She correctly recognized that his pornography habit was evil, and she was righteously concerned about his spiritual welfare. At the core, though, she also wanted to punish him and make him pay for the way he had hurt her. In that way, her motives were not pure. They were a mix of both righteous and unrighteous desires.

Of course, Ray also was not pure in heart. He too had an unrighteous desire that he had allowed to become a basic part of himself. That evil interest contradicted his otherwise righteous desires. It's interesting that in spite of his hypocrisy, he was able to function reasonably well outside of his marriage. In his marriage, however, it was much more difficult to hide the truth.

Therein lies one of the reasons purity of heart is so important in close relationships. Core values and motives become known and affect, or perhaps infect, our partner. This is true even when they involve essentially private and personal behavior. Most likely this is similar to how these core issues will play out in the eternities. There they will be known; and once known, they will affect others. That is perhaps one of the reasons that only the pure in heart will see God and be able to dwell in his presence.

> **And blessed are all the peacemakers, for they shall be called the children of God (3 Nephi 12:9).**

Most parents know how important peacemakers are in a family. Some children seem, almost by nature, to be quarrelsome and contentious. They take pleasure in teasing, complaining about, and generally upsetting their siblings. Imagine taking a long trip in a car with one or more such children in the group. It's not a pretty picture.

Peacemakers, on the other hand, are always welcome. They can take teasing in stride, without retaliating. They have the best interest of others at heart. They are appreciative and kind. Finding a car full of such children would probably be a miracle, but it would also be a pleasure, no matter how long the trip.

This attribute is critically important in marriage. In marriage, a quarrelsome, contentious nature is poisonous. Intimate relationships don't do well in an environment of whining, provoking, or quarreling. Being married under that condition might be compared to taking a long ride cooped up with rebellious, contentious children. It's not a lot of fun.

There are various reasons that some children are peacemakers and others are not, but that discussion is beyond the scope here. The same could be said for adults. With adults, however, choice most likely plays a dominant role. Contentious marriage partners are contentious because they make choices that lead them to be. They may insist, for instance, that justice be done, that things turn out fairly, or that their opinions be heard and respected. As discussed in earlier chapters, anytime we *require* certain behaviors from others, or *require* certain outcomes in our relationships, we set ourselves up for frustration.

No one can be a peacemaker unless he or she learns to give others the benefit of the doubt and unless he or she avoids trying to force his or her needs and interests on others. A clue as to the extent to which we reach this ideal in our marriage can be found in the honest answer to two self-assessment questions: (1) Who usually is first to try to resolve the problem when we have a disagreement? (2) Who usually gets his or her way when we disagree on a course of action? Biased perception may make it difficult to honestly answer these questions, but there is value in giving it a try anyway. You might also check your answers with your spouse's. A discussion of the subject could help each of you become more of a peacemaker.

> **And blessed are all they who are persecuted**
> **for my name's sake, for theirs is the kingdom**
> **of heaven (3 Nephi 12:10).**

Much of what has been written in prior chapters points to the need to live righteously in marriage, even when our partner doesn't do his or her part. Unfortunately, a partner will sometimes take advantage of a spouse who lives by this rule. The service-oriented spouse may end up doing most of the work in the marriage. A peacemaker married to someone selfish might end up too often having his or her needs and wishes ignored. Still, God's marriage manual suggests the need to do the right thing no matter what the consequence. Those who act righteously, even if their doing so contributes to poor treatment from others will ultimately be blessed for their good choices.

Acting righteously even if we have been treated unrighteously is particularly relevant in a situation in which one spouse seriously hurts the other. Tricia's husband was unfaithful to her with a woman he had met at work. He confessed his adultery and sought to keep his marriage together. For her part, Tricia had trouble knowing how to respond. She had questions such as "Should I welcome him back into my bed after what he has done?" "Should I trust him again even though he has proven to be untrustworthy?" "Should I treat him well, as if nothing has happened, after he has done this horrible thing to me?"

The eighth beatitude provides an answer for Tricia. As a believer in Christ, she should do the right thing no matter what her husband did or does. Infidelity is on the short list of justifiable reasons to end her marriage, and she might do that if so directed by the Spirit. This is generally not the best response, however, for all of the reasons cited in the previous chapter—especially in a situation in which her husband is repentant and wants to work things out. In staying married, the right thing is to trust her husband and treat him well. It might seem as though she is being naive or foolish to trust her husband and accept him back under the circumstances. But the Lord's promise is that she will be blessed for doing the right thing, even if her husband takes advantage of her righteous actions.

As long as she chooses to stay married, she should also choose to do all in her power to make the marriage work. By doing her best to treat her husband according to the Lord's commandments, she will be happier than she would be otherwise. Her marriage will have the best chance of surviving. And at the end of the day, she can feel good about herself and her effort in her marriage, even if her husband falls again. In short, she will ultimately be much better off by following the advice in God's marriage manual, even if the consequences of doing so are negative in the short run.

CHAPTER NINE

BECOME MORE UNSELFISH

——

Then said Jesus unto his disciples, If any man will come after me, let him deny himself, and take up his cross, and follow me.

MATTHEW 16:24

And now for a man to take up his cross, is to deny himself all ungodliness, and every worldly lust, and keep my commandments.

JST, MATTHEW 16:26

If we take up the cross as defined above, our goal will be to conform to God's marriage manual in all particulars. We will become forgiving, humble, nonjudgmental, positive-minded, and all of the good things described in previous chapters. We will also become unselfish. Or using the term in the scripture quoted above, we will develop the habit of *denying* ourselves.

Denying oneself, or being unselfish, took a bad rap in the popular psychology of the seventies. Those were the times when we were encouraged to stand up for ourselves and make ourselves number one. We were to avoid guilt at all costs, speak up when we had needs, and make sure others did not manipulate us. Unfortunately, going too far down that path results in selfishness, which is anathema in marriage. Perhaps that's one of the reasons for the soaring divorce rate in recent years.

It's interesting that at about the same time we were reading that we should put ourselves first, a prophet of God wrote a letter to a young couple who were contemplating divorce. His words, excerpted here, convey quite a different message: "I do know that two people as seemingly intelligent and apparently mature as you two, could have a gloriously happy life, if both of you would begin to let your concerns run in favor of the other, instead of in favor of your selfish selves. The escapist never escapes. If two people, selfish and self-centered, and without the spirit of forgiveness, escape from each other, they cannot escape from themselves. The disease is not cured by the separation or the divorce, and it will most assuredly follow along in the wake of future marriages. The cause must be removed" (Spencer W. Kimball, *The Miracle of Forgiveness* [1969], 271).

President Kimball further said, "Every divorce is the result of selfishness on the part of one or the other or both parties to a marriage contract. Someone is thinking of self-comforts, conveniences, freedoms, luxuries, or ease" (*The Teachings of Spencer W. Kimball* [1982], 313). Selfishness is at the root of divorce for the reasons President Kimball mentions and also because it's a root vice underlying other vices. Coveting, pride, anger, failing to forgive, and most other vices grow out of love of self. It's one of the great ironies that self-love ultimately guarantees self-destruction. Following are some areas in which self-ishness proves particularly destructive to a marriage relationship.

SELFISHNESS AND SEX

It's rare that a couple is sexually perfectly compatible. Or if they are generally compatible, it's not likely that they will always be. For one thing, the sexual drive varies from person to person, and even within the same person over time. For another, issues that come and go in family life affect one's interest in sex. Pressures resulting from work or child rearing are two of the most common such factors, and general health often plays a role as well. Furthermore, the quality of the relationship at any given moment is a strong determining factor. This leads to a common vicious circle in which one spouse who is interested in having sex is angry with the reluctant partner who is not. This anger is unsettling to the less-interested spouse who then finds it all the more difficult to be close physically. This in turn aggravates the needy spouse who becomes angrier still, and around it goes.

Unselfishness is the key to breaking this kind of vicious circle. On one side of it, the less-interested spouse can make the sexual relationship more of a priority. Interest in sex may not be there, but interest in meeting the needs of one's spouse can be. On the other side of it, the interested spouse can also unselfishly adjust his or her priorities and back off. We often speak in terms of sexual "need," but need is probably the wrong term. Certainly, it is not fatal if the sexual drive goes unexpressed.

The problem for those caught in this kind of vicious circle is that each partner tends to blame the other rather than focusing on his or her own selfishness. The less-interested spouse often takes a supposed moral high ground, suggesting that his or her partner is carnally minded and way out of line to make sex so important. This moralistic viewpoint may or may not be correct, but it certainly throws cold water on the relationship. The more-interested partner generally thinks of his or her spouse as lazy or insensitive. Some accuse the other of having a sexual hang-up of some kind. This also may or may not be true; but to suggest it certainly damages the relationship.

The good news is that when both partners act unselfishly, a compromise is achieved naturally and inevitably. Neither ends up feeling unloved or that he or she is being treated insensitively. Since this is always the case, if a couple experiences pain in their marriage because of sexual incompatibility, it's absolute evidence that one or both of them is acting selfishly. The pain would not be there otherwise. If this problem exists in your marriage, it's important to look at what *you* can do to act less selfishly. Unfortunately, those who are self-centered usually focus on what their partner needs to do for them, not vice versa. Take a close look at your thinking if you find yourself in this situation. If you dwell primarily on what your partner needs to do, the shoe might fit.

While on the subject, it should be noted that unselfishness can only work its magic when the needs of each partner are known. In some relationships, one partner feels slighted sexually but doesn't express the problem. Or the other partner feels sexually put upon and likewise doesn't say anything about it. Sex is one issue in marriage that needs to be periodically talked about. If either partner is unhappy in this department, he or she should speak up. It's also wise to occasionally quiz your partner regarding his or her comfort level in the physical relationship. Too often the big problems that can erupt over this issue come as a great surprise to one spouse or the other.

SELFISHNESS AND COMMUNICATION

To some, it may seem peculiar that though most couples rate communication as one of the most important issues in their marriage, it's a topic that's rarely addressed in the scriptures. The reason, I believe, has to do with the fact that communication problems are the result of selfishness or other inadequacies of virtue. When individuals are behaving according to the directions given in God's marriage manual, communication problems are rare and easily resolved.

This is particularly true with respect to selfishness. In his relationship with his wife, Ron was not a good listener. After a number of years of being frustrated by his behavior, Sheri convinced him to take a marriage class with her. She was excited when they got to the subject of reflective listening. Ron made positive comments in class and seemed to do well with the exercises. He definitely understood the technique, but nothing improved in his communication at home.

The class did little good because the problem was more basic than poor technique. Ron was so wrapped up in himself that Sheri's concerns were not important to him. He didn't listen well because he didn't care very much about what she had to say. Rather than trying to figure out where she was coming from, he interpreted her comments in terms of his needs. He also spent so much time focusing on what he was going to say, or entertaining his private thoughts, that he wasn't really able to hear what Sheri was saying.

The solution finally did come, but it was only after Ron began to recognize the real problem. He became humble enough to finally hear his wife's long-standing complaint. From there, he made a conscious effort to look outside himself. Some of his effort involved simple changes. He would make sure to put his book or magazine down when Sheri addressed him while he was reading. He frequently approached her just to talk, with no personal agenda. He engineered walks together and other unstructured times in which there was a maximum opportunity for communication.

When Sheri was talking, Ron also consciously kept reminding himself to ask: "What is she saying? What is she feeling? What is she really trying to say?" By simply focusing on these questions, the improvement in his listening skills was dramatic. It was just a matter of focus. Before, his focus had been on himself, what he wanted to say, and what he needed to have. That one-sided approach was obviously a barrier to effective communication. Now his focus had become what Sheri was saying and what she needed. He didn't ignore his own needs; he just changed the focus away from them. Effective communication became a given.

As he worked at becoming less self-centered, Ron also learned something else. He was happier! It seemed as though his wife was more in tune with his needs and more willing to give to him. He learned to apply the Lord's teachings on selflessness: "For whosoever will save his life shall lose it; but whosoever shall lose his life for my sake and the gospel's, the same shall save it" (Mark 8:35). The Lord was perhaps referring here to the possibility of gaining eternal life by those who are willing to sacrifice for Him (see JST, Mark 8:37–38), but His words also apply to the self-destructive nature of selfishness. Acquiring a fulfilling life depends in large part on losing ourselves in the service of others.

Before leaving Ron's example, something else is worth noting. After he became a better listener, Ron realized that he still wasn't a very good conversationalist. When analyzed, he realized this was primarily because he didn't think what he had to say was that important. If his thoughts were about work, he didn't think his wife would care or understand. If his thoughts were about nothing in particular, what value could there be in expressing them? This was a subtle form of self-centeredness. He was keeping to himself too much, no longer because of self-love, but now because he thought others wouldn't care.

He learned that he was wrong. Sheri did care. In fact, his reluctance to share seemed to her as though she wasn't important to him. It's significant that Ron came to this understanding through his newly acquired skill of being able to really listen to his wife. With this understanding, Ron made the decision to open up more about what was going on in his life, whether or not he thought his wife would understand or be interested. He also decided to think out loud more. If he and his wife were driving in the car somewhere, he would be more likely to share random thoughts, e.g., "I wonder how they made that bridge." or "That cloud looks like an elephant." He didn't expect his wife to respond, and comments such as these didn't necessarily go anywhere. But they had value because the mere act of sharing promoted intimacy and closeness between Ron and his wife.

For her part, Ron's wife also made changes that improved their ability to communicate. As are many other women, Ron's wife was naturally more open and willing than he to think out loud. So much so that over the years, she had been monopolizing airtime.

She needed to curb her natural tendency a little in order to give Ron room to open up.

In fact, Ron and Sheri discovered several differences between their communication habits. Some of these were the result of normal gender differences, others the product of personal tendencies. The key point, however, is that they were able to recognize and accommodate these differences once they were more in tune with the principles in God's marriage manual. By being more unselfish, more humble, and more loving, they were able to communicate more effectively, and their marriage was enhanced.

SELFISHNESS AND ROLE ENVY

This discussion has to do with what has unfortunately become less common in recent years—the traditional family in which Dad is the breadwinner and Mom stays home with the kids. In the traditional family, it's not uncommon for a young wife who has made the wise decision to stay home with the children to become a little jealous of the freedom her husband has. She may envy his daily association with adults and a schedule that seems to include doing challenging and interesting things. At the same time, the young husband may be a little jealous of what looks to him to be his wife's fair amount of discretionary time. This is especially true if he comes home unexpectedly to find his wife reading a book or watching TV during the children's naptimes.

Older couples may experience a similar problem, but usually it's the husband who is jealous. He may still be committed to a job for which he has perhaps lost enthusiasm, while his wife has, in fact, a great deal of discretionary time now that the kids are raised. The homemaker, in some cases, gets to retire a little earlier than the breadwinner does.

Jealousy in these cases is often a result of self-centered thinking. The young mother jealous of her husband's freedom is looking at the world through only her eyes. In the process she is underestimating the pressure her husband feels at work and how difficult his role is as breadwinner. Likewise, the young husband who is jealous of his wife's discretionary time is not seeing the significant pressure she is under being a full-time mother. If either husband or wife were to look outside of self to get an accurate picture of his or her partner's role in the family, he or she would have more respect for the other and certainly experience less role envy.

Jealousy in these cases results from selfishly looking only at the disadvantages of one's own role while overestimating the partner's advantages. When looked at unselfishly, meaning realistically, the fact is that the advantages and disadvantages of the different roles in marriage tend to balance out. This is true even of the case in which the homemaker is able to retire earlier than her husband is. She then receives a degree of compensation for the sacrifice she has made and the exceptionally demanding responsibility she has carried for so many years as a full-time mother and homemaker. Those were the years when her husband could leave on a business trip to Florida while she stayed home with the around-the-clock demands of sick children. Or if not so glamorous, the husband's job still offered opportunities to get some relief from pressing issues at home.

With an unselfish perspective, each spouse will be comfortable with his or her own role. And each spouse will appreciate the efforts of the other. Knowing that our efforts are appreciated is naturally an important ingredient in marriage. It allows each partner freedom to focus on doing the best job possible with respect to his or her individual role. It also leads to efforts to help one another. By viewing his wife's contributions in this way, a husband will do his share of child care and make sure that his wife has opportunities to meet her personal needs. A wife will do what she can to support her husband in his role and make sure that he also has the opportunity to meet his personal needs.

The idea of meeting personal needs is too often ignored in a relationship. A wife will assume that her husband has his needs met at work or elsewhere, and therefore expect too much from him in the way of taking over with the kids when he's home. "I've been with them all day, it's your turn!" Or the husband will feel that his wife has plenty of opportunity to meet personal needs and that she doesn't need his help. "You can get a baby-sitter and get out anytime you want. Get off my case!" This is an issue that deserves further discussion.

SELFISHNESS AND PERSONAL TIME

Selfishness with regard to the allocation of personal time has the potential to significantly mar a marriage, but it's sometimes hard to determine when selfishness is involved and who the guilty party is. For example, Jerry is a serious golfer. To maintain a competitive level he feels he needs to play regularly. Unfortunately, his work requires fifty to sixty hours a week, including his commute, and he also has a significant Church assignment. His wife, Andrea, and his three children also require time and attention. Something has to give, and when Jerry makes time for golf, Andrea thinks that it's the family that suffers. Jerry typically plays two to three times a month, and she sees that as way too often. Jerry, on the other hand, thinks of himself as being quite unselfish. He would enjoy playing golf several times a week if he could, so limiting his rounds to two or three times a month seems like a significant concession.

Selfishness is probably a factor here, but who is being the selfish one? Is it Jerry or is it Andrea? Perhaps Andrea is being selfish in requiring his help with the children or being jealous of his freedom, along the lines discussed in the previous section. Or maybe Jerry is being selfish in spending as much time as he does on golf. Two to three times a month may not sound like much, but it takes at least half a day each time he plays. That's a significant percentage of his discretionary time. Both Jerry and Andrea have supporters who see his or her point of view, and there is clearly no absolute right or wrong here.

The answer in this kind of situation probably depends on *both* spouses acting unselfishly. Given an unselfish attitude, Jerry's wife would go easy on pressuring Jerry to cut back on his golf. The worst thing she can do is make it a big deal in their relationship. She can ask for his cooperation, but the more that she pleads with him or lectures him on the need to be more committed to his family, the bigger the wedge she drives between them. Conversely, demonstrating an unselfish attitude would go a long way toward building their marriage.

If Jerry were to do the unselfish thing, he would be willing to give up golf altogether, or at least cut back even more than he already had. Notice the key word *willing*. If he limited his golf while acting the martyr, or if he did so simply because he felt he had to, there would be little benefit. He would likely resent his wife, and the overall effect in their relationship would be negative. Being *willing* to make that choice, on the other hand, would build their relationship without building resentment.

If both Jerry and Andrea were able to approach this problem unselfishly, they would be in position to find a compromise that would work for both of them. After all, they both have needs for recreation and personal fulfillment, and they are both committed to their family. On her side of it, Andrea would not demand that he give up golf. She might even encourage it since she knows how important it is to him. At the least she would generally be a supporter, a fan! She may not care about golf at all, but she presumably cares a great deal about her husband.

Likewise, Jerry would not in any way sacrifice his family to his hobby. He would also seek to discover and support Andrea's involvement in activities that are of equal personal interest to her. The result would be that Jerry and Andrea would meet somewhere in the middle. Interestingly, the actual ratio of golf to family time may or may not actually need to change in order to resolve the issue. The only thing that must change is attitude. As long as either Jerry or Andrea *thinks* that the other is being selfish, there is a problem. Along with behaving unselfishly, both Jerry and Andrea must avoid thinking negatively of the other.

SELFISHNESS AND BREATHING ROOM

Sometimes couples don't spend enough time together, and sometimes they spend too much. It's healthy when each partner feels free to pursue personal interests independent of his or her spouse. Of course, I'm talking about reasonable personal interests. I know one wife who thought her husband should be accepting of her weekly night out with her girlfriends. Most of her friends were single, and they made the rounds to dance clubs once a week. Her husband's concern was understandable. Naturally, it's also important that time spent in the pursuit of personal interests not be at the expense of time spent on family and on the marriage relationship, as discussed in the previous section.

With these constraints in mind, relationships seem to work best when each spouse is unselfishly supportive of his or her partner's involvement in personal interests.

I always wanted to be a pilot. My wife wasn't all that interested for herself, but she was supportive of the time and money required for me to get licensed and then pursue my hobby. When I held back, thinking that it was taking too much time or money, she was there cheering me on. I have known others with an equal interest in flying, and the means to do so, who would have had to pursue their dream over their wife's dead body. That's unfortunate.

My wife likes going to the theater much more than I do. I am supportive of her taking whatever time and money she wishes to pursue that interest with friends or other family members. She also will travel on her own when there is someplace she wants to go and it seems too expensive for both of us to take the trip or I'm not that interested in going. Certainly, a great relationship requires having shared experiences and spending time together, but it is also healthy when individual interests can be pursued without it being perceived as a threat to the marriage.

It takes an unselfish attitude to allow your spouse to spend time or money on something that's not of particular interest to you. It also takes an unselfish attitude to enjoy personal pursuits without requiring one's partner to participate. We certainly haven't solved all of our selfishness problems in our marriage; but at least my wife doesn't force me to go to the theater, and I don't force her to fly.

SELFISHNESS AND CONFLICT RESOLUTION

Many couples experience grief over issues related to how they spend their time and money. Some people are into sports or other hobbies in a way that offends their partner. Some buy things that their spouse thinks are unnecessary. Others insist on spending an amount of time with their extended family that seems excessive to their partner. Important issues that a couple must decide, such as the number of children to have and when to have them, can also cause trauma and conflict when differences of opinion exist. Whatever the issue, the fact is, two people can't share life without having differences of opinion.

Selfishness is the key in determining whether or not these differences of opinion result in conflict. Difference of opinion + selfishness = conflict. If this formula is understood, it gives a couple an important place to begin in resolving conflicts in their marriage. The questions become, "Am I acting selfishly in this situation?" "What can I do to meet my spouse at least half way?" Notice that the questions aren't asking whether your *partner* is acting selfishly. That's something you can't productively do anything about, even if it is so.

If your best effort to resolve an issue unselfishly doesn't seem to work or if your points of conflict are especially difficult, you might try a formal conflict resolution strategy. One such strategy involves the following simple steps:

STEP 1: Each spouse states his or her wishes in the situation.

STEP 2: Each spouse repeats back the feelings of his or her partner to the other's satisfaction.

STEP 3: The couple then brainstorms for solutions that could work for both partners.

STEP 4: A solution acceptable to both partners is selected for trial run.

STEP 5: If the trial isn't successful to both partners, a new solution is found and tried.

As an example of how this works, consider the problem faced by Sam and Linda. Sam is an accountant who keeps meticulous financial records and who tries to carefully budget the family resources. Linda is not interested in balancing checkbooks, and she has a hard time living according to a budget. If the family needs groceries, she buys groceries. If clothes are needed, she buys clothes. She isn't really a spendthrift, she just doesn't keep good track of expenditures, and she doesn't discipline herself to live within a budget.

Sam and Linda decided to try the steps in conflict resolution outlined above. First, they identified for each other the problem and their feelings in the situation. Sam felt financially responsible for the family, yet he was frustrated in reaching the family's financial goals. Linda agreed with those goals but then didn't do the things Sam believed were necessary to accomplish them. For her part, Linda felt controlled and accused. She believed Sam thought of her as a selfish spendthrift, when she was not. She also felt as though Sam was treating her like one of the children whenever he lectured her, which he frequently did. Budgets and checkbooks just weren't her thing anyway.

Accomplishing step 2 of the process proved to be a little difficult, but they got through it. In step 2 it was necessary to repeat back to the other what his or her partner felt in the situation. This was to be done to the partner's satisfaction and without editorializing. It took several attempts by each of them to be able to express the other's view accurately and without commenting on how right or wrong they thought it was.

In step 3 they came up with a plan they hoped would work. They agreed to establish two separate funds—one for each of them to control. Expenditures from those funds would not need to be justified to the other. They also established a spending limit beyond which they would not go without the approval of the other. Further, Sam agreed that he would not lecture Linda, nor would he require her to balance her checkbook. Linda agreed to make sure the amount was recorded each time she wrote a check, and to turn the checkbook over to Sam monthly for reconciliation. Finally, they agreed to review family finances weekly.

They then implemented their plan (step 4) and found that it worked reasonably well. It became clear, however, that the extent to which it worked depended on how unselfish they were. Sam had to largely give up his hope that family finances could be meticulously monitored and controlled. Otherwise, he found it impossible not to be critical of Linda's purchases and occasional carelessness in recording. She was doing better in response to their plan, but she certainly wasn't operating to his standard. Linda had to give up her tendency to spend without accounting for her expenditures. It took an unselfish effort on her part to do something that didn't come naturally and that she really didn't think was that important in the first place.

Sam and Linda discovered that by each giving up some of what they wanted, they ended up getting more of what they wanted. Not only did their relationship improve, but they also found their partner to be more willing to meet their needs. This result is an example of the seeming paradox described by the Lord and quoted earlier: "For whosoever will save his life shall lose it; but whosoever shall lose his life for my sake and the gospel's, the same shall save it" (Mark 8:35). If we are to gain a fulfilling life or a fulfilling marriage, we must lose ourselves in the service of others.

CHAPTER TEN

GOD'S INSTRUCTIONS SUMMARIZED

———

The reader who has stuck with me this far hopefully sees how the scriptures truly constitute the best marriage manual available. Practicing the principles taught therein will provide any couple a fulfilling relationship. Failure to comply will inevitably result in conflict, pain, and distress. It's also true that a couple need to attempt to comply with *all* the principles taught in scripture. As you have probably noticed, the virtues taught are interrelated. Several, if not all, play into each of the real-life examples presented in this book. In the last case of Sam and Linda, for example, the primary virtue illustrated is the need to be unselfish.

Actually, each of the principles discussed in the chapters of this book is also important. Learning to forgive, controlling anger, being humble, striving not to covet, being nonjudgmental, thinking positively, remembering love, keeping covenants, practicing patience, and living the Beatitudes are all needed to resolve Sam and Linda's problem. Each scriptural attribute plays a part in determining whether or not these two will move on to have a great marriage.

Since they are all important, each of the principles discussed in the book is summarized below. Page numbers are given where a discussion of the principle begins in this book; but more important, a scriptural reference or two is also provided. Keep in mind that the principle may be discussed in more than one place in this book and that other scriptural references exist for most principles cited. The citations given are to be considered basically as a starting point for further investigation.

You might also find it useful to review each of the principles summarized, asking yourself how well you are doing with respect to each one—sort of a self-test of character. If you are really brave, you might also have your spouse critique your behavior in relationship to the divine standards. As you do either of these things, keep in mind the unique promise made to those who diligently search for the truths taught in God's marriage manual: "If ye shall ask with a sincere heart, with real intent, having faith in Christ, he will manifest the truth of it unto you, by the power of the

Holy Ghost. And by the power of the Holy Ghost ye may know the truth of all things" (Moroni 10:4).

PRINCIPLE

Perfection in the practice of tolerance, patience, long-suffering and love is more important than perfection in filling assignments and performing duties. Page 4. 1 Corinthians 13:1-3.

PRINCIPLE

One must be continually forgiving of both serious and less serious offenses, whether or not the offender "deserves" forgiveness. Page 7. Matthew 18:21-22.

PRINCIPLE

If we truly forgive, we may remember the offense, but the memory is no longer painful. Page 10. Alma 36:19-20.

PRINCIPLE

We need to forgive, even if principle is on our side, even if it feels as though we are letting the other person get away with something, and even if doing so doesn't seem fair. Page 17. D&C 64:8-10.

PRINCIPLE

We need to clearly identify the problem to whom-ever offends us whenever we are offended, and to do so privately. Page 24. Matthew 18:15.

PRINCIPLE

We need to pray for strength to meet difficult chal-lenges. Page 27. Matthew 17:21.

PRINCIPLE

We must be slow to anger in family situations. Page 31. Proverbs 15:18.

PRINCIPLE

If we have contention and anger in our hearts, we are being influenced by the devil. Page 32. 3 Nephi 11:29-30.

PRINCIPLE

Even good cause doesn't justify our anger. Page 34. Compare Matthew 5:22 with 3 Nephi 12:22.

PRINCIPLE

We are much better off trying to suppress anger than venting it. Page 35. *Journal of Discourses* 11:255.

PRINCIPLE

In the interest of moral agency, we must not create situations in which we demand that someone else behaves in a certain way. Page 41. 2 Nephi 2:27.

PRINCIPLE

We set ourselves up for frustration and anger when we try to do too much at once. Page 44. Mosiah 4:27.

PRINCIPLE

It's important that we be willing to learn from our spouse and others. Page 49. 1 Peter 5:5.

PRINCIPLE

It's important to respect your partner's opinion, even if you disagree about an important issue. Page 56. 1 Corinthians 7:3.

PRINCIPLE

It's critical that we treat each other with courtesy and respect, which happens naturally if we truly are humble. Page 56. Matthew 7:12.

PRINCIPLE

We must be willing to admit when we are wrong. Page 58. James 5:16.

PRINCIPLE

Healthy relationships require that each partner serves the other. Page 60. Matthew 20:25-27.

PRINCIPLE

We need to serve others and treat them kindly, even if we think they don't deserve to be treated well. Page 62. Matthew 5:39-41.

PRINCIPLE

We are coveting whenever we want something (time, warmth, attention, sex, agreement, or whatever) so badly that we are willing to break the rules to

get it or when we can't be happy without it. Page 67.
Exodus 20:17.

PRINCIPLE

Letting ourselves desire, yearn for, or crave a
romantic relationship outside of our marriage is a
huge mistake. Page 72. Spencer W. Kimball, in
Conference Report, October 1962, 58-59.

PRINCIPLE

No matter how innocent our thoughts may seem,
coveting another relationship is a dangerous sin. Page
77. Matthew 5:28.

PRINCIPLE

Material possessions will not bring happiness and
coveting them will cause problems in family relationships. Page 81. Luke 12:15-21.

PRINCIPLE

We must focus only on our own problems, not
those of our spouse. Page 83. Matthew 7:1-5.

PRINCIPLE

We need to make righteous judgments about moral issues and what our response to moral questions will be, but we must avoid unrighteous judgments. In marriage, unrighteous judgments include giving too much advice, or generally being too critical. Page 86. Matthew 7:1-2 and JST Matthew 7:1-2.

PRINCIPLE

Rather than trying to motivate by criticizing and withholding acceptance, we need to motivate with love. Page 99. John 15:10.

PRINCIPLE

It's important to focus on what's right, not on what's wrong about others and ourselves. Page 101. 3 Nephi 13:22-23 and John 8:10-11.

PRINCIPLE

Family life should be approached cheerfully, even when things aren't going well. Page 103. D&C 123:17.

PRINCIPLE

Avoid dogmatic, absolute statements about issues other than eternal truths. Page 109. 3 Nephi 12:33-37.

PRINCIPLE

Think positively by focusing on eternal opportunities, even when things in the present are negative. Page 112. Hebrews 10:34 and D&C 84:37-38.

PRINCIPLE

Think of problems as temporary, not permanent—"this too shall pass." Think of problems as limited in scope, not pervasive—"this doesn't affect everything." Page 113. 1 Corinthians 15:22 and Isaiah 1:18.

PRINCIPLE

Focusing on a relationship, even though it may seem like a waste of time, is sometimes more important than attending to duties and responsibilities. Page 115. Luke 10:38-42.

PRINCIPLE

Since thoughts are so important in controlling

feelings and behavior, we need to be aware of what we are thinking. The Holy Ghost can help us do this. Page 118. D&C 50:14.

PRINCIPLE

The most important form of love in marriage is love as defined in the scriptures; namely, serving, being patient, and being long-suffering. Page 119. John 13:34-35.

PRINCIPLE

What we sometimes define as romantic love can really be lust or a love of worldly things. Page 123. 1 John 2:15.

PRINCIPLE

Physical attraction is not that important in this life and will become a nonissue altogether in the next. Page 124. Brigham Young, *Contributor* 9:240.

PRINCIPLE

Even those of us who are not naturally loving can learn to be so. Page 125. Proverbs 23:7. Spencer W. Kimball, *The Teachings of Spencer W. Kimball*, 245-46.

PRINCIPLE

Marriage is a sacred covenant between two people and between those two and God. Page 125. D&C 132:19.

PRINCIPLE

Divorcing because one falls out of love or was never in love in the first place or has fallen in love with someone else or has become tired of one's mate is not justified. Page 130. Joseph Fielding Smith, *Doctrines of Salvation,* 2:80.

PRINCIPLE

Those who break their marriage covenant will face problems in the next world. Page 134. D&C 84:41.

PRINCIPLE

Those who decide not to make the marriage covenant in the first place may lose their exaltation. Page 134. D&C 84:42 and D&C 132:21.

PRINCIPLE

Patience is required while we wait for our partner to grow into his or her potential and while we wait for our marriage relationship to reach its potential. Page 135. Hebrews 12:1 and Joseph F. Smith, *Gospel Doctrine*, 298.

PRINCIPLE

We are responsible to teach our children the truth, not force them to comply with it. Page 139. D&C 68:25 and Moses 4:3.

PRINCIPLE

We need to be humble enough to follow God's direction even when it conflicts with our personal desires. Page 144. 3 Nephi 12:3.

PRINCIPLE

It's necessary to mourn for our sins or, in other words, have "godly sorrow." Page 147. 2 Corinthians 7:10.

PRINCIPLE

We need to listen to and support those who are hurting, not give them advice or condemn them. Page 148. Mosiah 18:9.

PRINCIPLE

In family relationships, it is essential we be hard to provoke or irritate and that we be forgiving. Page 151. 3 Nephi 12:5.

PRINCIPLE

Doing the right thing, no matter what the consequence, needs to be our primary motive. Page 152. 3 Nephi 12:6.

PRINCIPLE

We need to emphasize mercy and leave justice to the Lord. Page 154. 3 Nephi 12:7.

PRINCIPLE

Our core values, beliefs, and motives must all be righteous. Page 156. 3 Nephi 12:8.

PRINCIPLE

Whining, provoking, and quarreling have no place in our marriage or family relationships. Page 158. 3 Nephi 12:9.

PRINCIPLE

We need to do the right thing in marriage, even if it seems as though our partner takes advantage of us for doing so. Page 159. 3 Nephi 12:10.

PRINCIPLE

Selfishness is almost certainly involved if we have pain in our marriage. Page 164. Spencer W. Kimball, *Miracle of Forgiveness*, 271.

PRINCIPLE

By giving up some of what we think we need, we end up getting more of what we really do need. Page 170. Mark 8:35.

The number of principles summarized above might seem a little overwhelming. Not only that, there are a number of others that could be included. The good news is that most of us are probably already successfully living the majority of these principles. Our efforts can therefore be directed to the relatively few places where we need improvement.

As mentioned earlier, there is also a unique and wonderful adjunct available to God's marriage manual. With prayer, humility, and dedicated focus we can know where to concentrate our efforts. In addition, we can also receive inspiration regarding how to go about applying these principles based on our own personal situations. Then we can receive real-time assistance as we attempt to live righteously.

It is my hope and prayer that the stories and ideas included in this book will help us all live closer to the ideal summarized by the prophet Alma: "And now I would that ye should be humble, and be submissive and gentle; easy to be entreated; full of patience and long-suffering; being temperate in all things; being diligent in keeping the commandments of God at all times; asking for whatsoever things ye stand in need, both spiritual and temporal; always returning thanks unto God for whatsoever things ye do receive. And see that ye have faith, hope, and charity, and then ye will always abound in good works" (Alma 7:23–24).

INDEX